Battle Orders · 10

OSPREY
PUBLISHING

US Tank and Tank Destroyer Battalions in the ETO 1944–45

Steven J Zaloga · *Consultant editor Dr Duncan Anderson*

Series editors Marcus Cowper and Nikolai Bogdanovic

First published in Great Britain in 2005 by Osprey Publishing, Elms Court,
Chapel Way, Botley, Oxford OX2 9LP, United Kingdom.
Email: info@ospreypublishing.com

ISBN 1 84176 798 0

Editorial by Ilios Publishing, Oxford, UK (www.iliospublishing.com)
Design: Bounford.com, Royston, UK
Maps by Bounford.com, Royston, UK
Index by Alan Thatcher
Originated by The Electronic Page Company, Cwmbran, UK
Printed and bound by L-Rex Printing Company Ltd

05 06 07 08 09   10 9 8 7 6 5 4 3 2 1

A CIP catalog record for this book is available from the British Library.

FOR A CATALOGUE OF ALL BOOKS PUBLISHED BY OSPREY PLEASE CONTACT:

NORTH AMERICA
Osprey Direct, 2427 Bond Street, University Park, IL 60466, USA
E-mail: info@ospreydirectusa.com

ALL OTHER REGIONS
Osprey Direct UK, P.O. Box 140, Wellingborough,
Northants, NN8 2FA, UK
E-mail: info@ospreydirect.co.uk

www.ospreypublishing.com

Author's note

The photos in this book are primarily from the wartime US
Army's Signal Corps collections at the US National Archives and
Record Administration (NARA) in College Park, MD. Other
Signal Corps photos were located at other army facilities, and the
author would like to thank Randy Hackenburg and Jay Graybeal of
the special collections branch of the Military History Institute for
their help as well as Charles Lemons and Candace Fuller of the
Patton Museum at Ft. Knox.

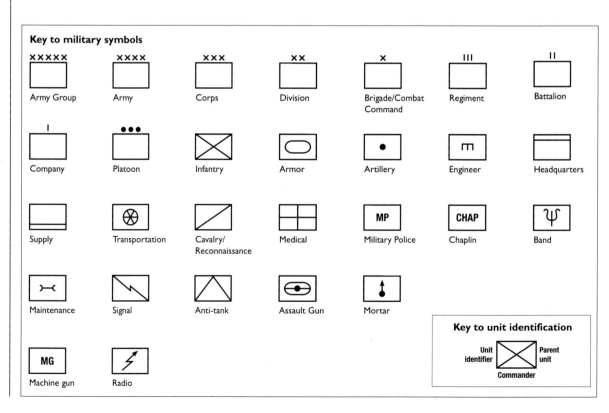

Key to military symbols

×××××	Army Group
××××	Army
×××	Corps
××	Division
×	Brigade/Combat Command
III	Regiment
II	Battalion
I	Company
•••	Platoon
Infantry	
Armor	
Artillery	
Engineer	
Headquarters	
Supply	
Transportation	
Cavalry/Reconnaissance	
Medical	
MP Military Police	
CHAP Chaplin	
Band	
Maintenance	
Signal	
Anti-tank	
Assault Gun	
Mortar	
MG Machine gun	
Radio	

Key to unit identification

Unit identifier / Parent unit / Commander

Contents

Introduction

Overshadowed by the United States Army's armored divisions, the separate tank and tank destroyer battalions had the difficult mission of providing armored support for US infantry divisions in the 1944–45 campaigns. Although infantry support had been the traditional role of US tanks in World War I, there was considerable controversy about US tank doctrine through World War II. Tank destroyers were a new concept first established in 1941, and ultimately an unsuccessful one. The tactical doctrine for tank destroyers was so flawed that the numerous tank destroyer battalions deployed in Europe in 1944–45 were not used as intended, but instead were assigned an infantry support mission similar to that of the separate tank battalions.

Infantry support had been the traditional mission of tanks since their birth in World War I. The vulnerability of exposed infantry to the lethal weapons of the modern battlefield led to static trench warfare. The infantry could not advance in the face of overwhelming enemy firepower and tanks arose as a means to break this stalemate. The tank could survive against machine guns and indirect artillery fire, and facilitate the advance of the infantry by knocking out machine-gun nests and tenacious defensive positions. Tanks helped even the odds in favor of the attacking infantry over the previously dominant defense.

A classic image of tank support in World War II. An M4 medium tank of the 746th Tank Battalion supports Co. I, 60th Infantry, 9th Infantry Division, during fighting near the Belgian border on September 9, 1944. (NARA)

Every new tactical innovation prompts a response, and the growing influence of tanks on the battlefield after 1918 led to various attempts to repel the tank threat. During World War I, anti-tank methods were improvised and awkward. Field guns were deployed in the forward trenches but every gun removed from the artillery role diminished the division's artillery firepower. Furthermore, these field guns were large, conspicuous, and vulnerable, and there were seldom enough available to halt a concentrated tank attack. In the inter-war years, new approaches were made to deal with the tank threat. The best solution was a dedicated anti-tank gun, small enough to be easily moved by the infantry, but powerful enough to deal with most tanks. The most influential of these weapons was the German Rheinmetall 37mm gun, which was first used extensively in the Spanish Civil War.

Although anti-tank guns proved to be very effective against the small numbers of tanks deployed in Spain in 1937–38, the evolution of tank tactics undermined their effectiveness. Instead of viewing the tank simply as an infantry support weapon, visionary military thinkers in the 1930s began to see tank divisions as a means to reinvigorate the offensive and return mobility to the battlefield. Since armored divisions could concentrate large numbers of tanks against a single point, for example a regiment of tanks against an infantry battalion, the small number of anti-tank guns available to the infantry would inevitably be overwhelmed. The inability of infantry anti-tank guns to ensure a defense against tank attack was made very evident during Germany's invasion of Poland in 1939, and even more clearly in the stunning defeat of the French Army in 1940.

If the infantry anti-tank gun could not provide a sufficient barrier against the tank threat, then what could do so? This was a critical tactical dilemma for most armies during World War II, and a dilemma that was never entirely solved. Some armies, such as Britain's, viewed armored divisions as being the best antidote to German panzer divisions. The Germans eventually relied on a blend of infantry anti-tank weapons, bolstered by a divisional assault-gun battalion. The US Army came up with its own solution, the Tank Destroyer Force, a semi-independent combat arm deployed specifically to deal with the panzer threat.

Combat mission

The tank battalion

During the interwar years from 1920 to 1939, the US Army maintained a very modest tank force as part of its infantry branch. At the same time, the cavalry maintained a separate armored force, but their cavalry tanks were euphemistically named "combat cars" since Congress had restricted the deployment of "tanks" to the infantry. The small size of the tank force was due in part to the very modest defense budget of the 1930s, as well as the strategic posture of the army. Due to America's isolationist foreign policy, it was presumed that the US Army would not become entangled in another major war in Europe. The focus of the army was homeland defense and policing the colonies and overseas possessions such as the Philippines, missions that did not require a large armored force.

For most of the 1930s, the US Army had a nominal order of battle of two tank regiments, the 66th and 67th Infantry (Light Tanks) and seven organic tank companies attached to infantry divisions. In reality, the only active element of the tank regiments was a single tank company, Company F, 67th Infantry (Light Tanks) at the infantry school at Ft. Benning, Georgia. Not counting experimental types, the US Army procured only 321 light tanks from 1930 to 1939, and the cavalry a further 148 combat cars.

The first of the new separate tank battalions was the 70th Tank Battalion. Company C, equipped with M3 light tanks, is seen here during training near Baldrushagi, Iceland, on May 3, 1942. (NARA)

The Spanish Civil War forced the US Army to reconsider its tank policy. The conflict made it clear that tanks would in the future be an important element in any major war, even in a war involving rag-tag militias such as Spain. In 1939, the US Army began to shift its infantry doctrine, no longer favoring the use of penny-packets of tanks in company-sized formations for infantry support, but instead shifting to the massed use of tanks with the battalion as the basic tactical unit. As a result, the scattered divisional tank companies were consolidated as the 68th Infantry Regiment (Tank), and in January 1940 they were all moved to the infantry school at Ft. Benning.

When war broke out in Europe in September 1939, the US Army realized that its basic strategic premise that it would not fight again in a major European conflict might no longer be valid. The successful use of massed panzer formations in Poland in 1939 led both the US infantry and the cavalry to begin to experiment with larger armor formations. A Provisional Tank Brigade was created at Ft. Benning in January 1940, and new armored units were tested during army maneuvers in Louisiana that year. The defeat of the French Army in May–June 1940 was a profound shock to US Army commanders. The French defeat, as well as the 1939–40 experiments led to a decision on July 10, 1940, to combine the major mechanized elements of the infantry and cavalry into a new combat arm, the Armored Force, headquartered at Ft. Knox, Kentucky. These units constituted the core of the new 1st Armored Division. The French defeat seemed to discredit the idea of scattering the tanks in separate tank battalions attached to the infantry, as the Germans had concentrated nearly all of their tanks in the panzer divisions. In contrast, the defeated French had scattered much of their armor among infantry and cavalry formations. US Army tank policy rapidly swung from its previous practice of separate tank battalions to a concentration of the armored force. As a result, the primary focus of the new Armored Force was the creation of the new armored divisions. The tactical doctrine of these new formations was heavily flavored by the cavalry who saw the armored divisions as a modern incarnation of the cavalry force, oriented towards a mobile exploitation role and not an infantry breakthrough role.

There were dissenting views and the chief of the infantry, Gen. George Lynch, insisted that the infantry still needed tank support to conduct their mission. The War Department approved the formation of new tank battalions alongside the new armored divisions, but at first these were very few in number. They were originally called GHQ tank battalions since they were envisioned as separate battalions assigned to the new General Headquarters (GHQ) that had been formed on July 26, 1940. In keeping with the new concept of the use of tanks en masse, these battalions were not organic to the infantry divisions but would be assigned at army or corps level to carry out specific missions, which might include some distribution to the infantry division for support, but which could also be used for independent missions or to reinforce the new armored divisions. Clearly, the pendulum had swung away from the infantry support mission.

Since the chief of the infantry was preoccupied with the need to form, train, and equip large numbers of new infantry divisions, the Armored Force dominated decisions on tank formations. The decision to rely first on the M3 light tank, and after 1942 on the M4 medium tank, was largely due to the suitability of these designs for Armored Force doctrine. Distracted by more pressing issues, the chief of infantry never paid much attention to the need for a specific infantry support tank akin to British infantry tanks such as the Matilda and Churchill, the Soviet KV and IS heavy tanks, or the German Tiger. As a result, the separate tank battalions were equipped with the same types of tanks and equipment as the battalions of the armored divisions, which tended to place a greater premium on mobility than on armored protection. Infantry support tanks such as the T14 that were developed for British Lend-Lease requirements were not accepted for US Army use.

The first of the new infantry tank battalions, the 70th Tank Battalion, was formed at Ft. Meade, Maryland, on July 15, 1940, from the troops of the 1st Battalion, 67th Armored Regiment. This was the only separate tank battalion until four more were formed (191st–194th Tank Battalions) in December 1940–March 1941, using tank companies from National Guard infantry divisions.

Since the army planned to use the GHQ tank battalions en masse, there was a need for a higher tactical headquarters to coordinate their operations. During 1941, the Army began the formation of the first tank groups with the activation of the 1st Tank Group (GHQ Reserve) at Ft. Knox on February 11 and the 2nd Provisional Tank Group at Camp Bowie, Texas, on March 1, 1941. The role of the Tank Group was to serve as a tactical and administrative headquarters for the several tank battalions attached to a corps or army. By July 1942 the number of tank groups had risen to five (1, 3, 5, 6, 7). The tank groups originally contained as many as five battalions, but it quickly became apparent that this was too many for its limited staff and so the composition was reduced to two or three. Later, most of the tank groups were renamed as armored groups since they could administer mixed units including both tank and armored infantry battalions. Ten new tank battalions were formed in June 1941 (751st–760th Tank Battalions), six as medium tank battalions (751st–755th) equipped with the new

The essential mission of separate tank battalions in the ETO was the support of infantry in close combat. Here, GIs of the 9th Division prepare to move forward on February 27, 1945, with a pair of M4A3E2 assault tanks of the 746th Tank Battalion. That day, the division finally captured one of the Roer dams at Schwammenauel. (NARA)

M3 medium tank, and the remainder in the usual light tank configuration, equipped with the M3 light tank. By the end of 1941, the number of GHQ tank battalions had risen to 15. The first of the new tank battalions to enter combat were the 192nd and 194th Tank Battalions, which formed the core of the Provisional Tank Group sent to the Philippines in the autumn of 1941. These units were overwhelmed with the rest of the US Army in the Philippines in April 1942 and their operations had little influence on evolving army doctrine.

In March 1942, the short-lived General Headquarters evolved into the Headquarters, Army Ground Forces (AGF). The chief of the AGF was Maj. Gen. Lesley McNair who became the architect of the wartime US Army. He was instrumental in raising, training, and equipping the divisions. McNair favored lean, modular combat formations that would be easier to ship overseas. Once in theater, the divisions could be tailored to local needs by the addition of specialized battalions such as tank, antiaircraft, engineer, and tank destroyer battalions. The tank group fitted neatly into his plans. Although the AGF under Gen. McNair and the Armored Force under Gen. Jacob Devers seldom saw eye-to-eye, they both agreed on the need for the tank groups. The Armored Force pushed for the tank group idea since they had plans to deploy tank groups as mini-armored divisions, not broken up in penny-packets for infantry support. As it would transpire in 1944–45, the flexibility and potential of the tank groups proved to be illusory and their drawbacks far outweighed their benefits. The other alternative would have been to deploy the tank battalions as an organic element of each infantry division, but this approach seemed to have been discredited by the 1939–41 blitzkrieg campaigns. The US Army was slow to appreciate that armored force tactics were evolving in the European war from the tank-heavy focus of the 1939–41 blitzkrieg campaigns to a new combined-arms approach. Both the German and Soviet armies gradually recognized that the infantry needed tank support and by 1942–43, both armies regularly attached tanks or assault-gun units to the infantry for close combat support.

The formation of new tank battalions was slow through 1942, since most of the focus was on creating new armored divisions. Only 14 more battalions were added in 1942, bringing the total to 27 after the loss of two in the Philippines. The separate tank battalions attracted so little attention that in early 1942 Devers remarked that "the tank battalions are now in the category of lost children and that we must take prompt action to bring them into the fold and be in closer touch with their needs and problems." Tank battalions were first committed to action in the Mediterranean theater at the end of 1942. Elements of the 70th and 756th Tank Battalions were deployed to North Africa in November 1942 as part of Operation Torch. Four more tank battalions were deployed to North Africa in January–March 1943 (751st, 752nd, 755th, 757th) along with two tank groups (1st and 2nd). Of these units, only the 70th and 751st saw extensive combat.

During February 1943, German units staged a counterattack against scattered US Army infantry and tank units, breaking through their defensive line and causing heavy losses. Although the German breakthrough was stopped, the fighting around Kasserine Pass made it clear that the US Army had to improve its training, tactics, and unit organization. The tank group concept was flawed. The infantry division commanders wanted direct tank support for their units, and there was little use for a pseudo-armored division when there were actual armored divisions present in theater to carry out large-scale armored operations. The light tank battalions were highly critical of the reliance on M3 and M5 tanks that were too poorly armored and too weakly armed to survive on the modern battlefield. Before any action could be taken on these lessons, US forces took part in Operation Husky on Sicily. Two separate tank battalions that had fought in North Africa, the 70th (Light) and 753rd (Medium) Tank Battalions were also deployed on Sicily.

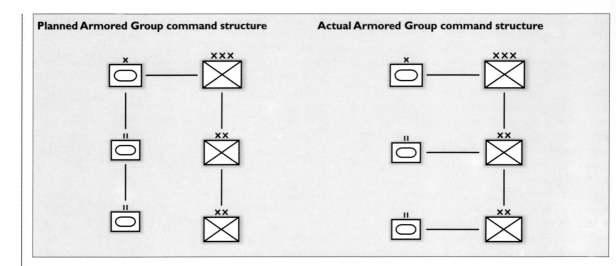

Planned Armored Group command structure

Actual Armored Group command structure

The actions fought in Tunisia and Sicily showed that more attention had to be paid to tank support for the infantry divisions. The tactic of using the separate tank battalions en masse was unsound since a true combined-arms unit like the armored division was more suited for those tasks. In addition, the infantry division commanders were unanimous in their need for close tank support. At the same time, combined-arms training of infantry and tank units had been neglected, in part due to the rush to create new divisions, and in part due to the doctrinal neglect of the need for infantry tank support. Infantry commanders frequently had received no training on how best to employ tanks when they were assigned, and often used them for inappropriate missions. In August 1942, prior to the Tunisia operation, McNair came up with plans to attach separate tank battalions to armies and corps for combined training. Although this scheme was generally accepted, practical problems meant that little was done. In March 1943, the AGF operations officer, Brig. Gen. John Lentz, argued that the separate tank battalions were a bad idea and that the tank units should be made organic to the infantry divisions. McNair opposed this idea, as he still clung to the idea that the non-divisional battalions would provide a vital mass of firepower and maneuver in the forthcoming campaign in France. McNair issued a directive in April 1943 stressing the need for more combined training by tank and infantry units. But tank battalions were still too few in number to permit each infantry division to train with a tank battalion and they were seldom located together at the same base. In June 1943, Maj. Gen. Walton Walker, commander of IV Armored Corps, returned from Tunisia and urged that separate tank battalions, after receiving basic unit training, be stationed with a corresponding infantry division for further training, and remain with that division during entry into combat. In the summer of 1943, Gen. Devers was appointed to head US forces in the new European Theater of Operations (ETO), and Lt. Gen. Alvan Gillem became the Armored Force commander. In July 1943, Gillem visited US units on Sicily and came back convinced that more attention had to be paid to the specific requirements of tank–infantry cooperation. In spite of McNair's opposition, there was gathering momentum to shift the mission from the massed use of separate tank battalions to support the corps or army, to the dispersed use of the battalions to directly support infantry divisions. The pendulum had swung back again to the traditional role of these units.

In September 1943, the armored division was reorganized with a better balance of tanks, armored infantry, and armored field artillery, ending up with three battalions of each. Since the previous organization of the armored division included two armored regiments with three tank battalions each, this left a surplus of three tank battalions from each of the reorganized divisions. These surplus tank battalions were earmarked as separate tank battalions. In addition to new battalions created in 1943, this expanded the US Army's tank force from 27 to 70 separate tank battalions by the end of 1943.

Lessons from the North African campaign also led to significant organizational changes in the tank battalions. Prior to the 1943 organization, tank battalions were configured either as light or medium tank battalions, equipped solely with light or medium tanks. The North African campaign had made it clear that the days of the light tanks were over and that the medium tank had become the centerpiece of the tank battalion. Although many armor officers recommended abandoning the light tank entirely in favor of medium tanks, AGF was unwilling to do so since there were so many of the new M5A1 light tanks available. The AGF argued that the light tanks could still perform a useful function in the battalion such as scouting and flank security. As a result, a new tank battalion organization was developed consisting of three medium tank companies (Cos. A, B, C) and one light tank company (Co. D). There were some exceptions to this rule. A few separate tank battalions retained a homogenous light tank organization, though the reasons for that remain obscure. Both the separate tank battalions and those belonging to the armored divisions followed a common table of organization and equipment (TO&E) with the exception of the rare light tank battalions. The September 1943 changes were the last major reorganization of the separate tank battalions prior to the start of the campaign in the ETO.

The AGF sent out a new directive to corps commanders on October 16, 1943, stressing the need for more combined training of tanks and infantry but later inspections revealed that too little was being done. In April 1944 Gen. Gillem

During the final campaign in Germany, tanks were frequently used to make infantry task forces more mobile. An M4A3 with a squad of infantry on the back moves through Weitzlar on March 28, 1945. (NARA)

organized a conference of senior commanders at Ft. Benning in April 1944 to demonstrate proper tank–infantry tactics. Unfortunately, few of the tank battalions committed to combat in France in the summer of 1944 had received proper tank–infantry training due to the belated recognition of this key mission.

The tank destroyer battalion

Dealing with the threat of massed panzer attack became one of the US Army's top priorities in 1940–41. At the beginning of the war, each US Army infantry battalion had three 37mm anti-tank guns, each regiment had 18, and each division had 54. As became evident in the 1939–40 campaigns in Europe, cordon defense using infantry anti-tank guns spread thinly along the main-line-of-resistance could not stop the advance of panzer divisions since the concentrated mass of armor would usually overcome the few anti-tank guns in that sector by sheer weight of numbers. To stiffen the anti-tank cordon, in October 1940, the heavy howitzer battalion in each US infantry division was reinforced with an anti-tank gun battery with eight 75mm anti-tank guns. Wargames suggested that more was needed, so on July 24, 1941, the War Department ordered the activation of an anti-tank battalion in each division. This battalion included the eight 75mm guns formerly in the artillery battalion, reinforced by two more companies of the new 37mm guns. In addition to the divisional battalions, the army began to form separate anti-tank battalions under GHQ control. Several of these were used in the Louisiana wargames in the autumn of 1941.

The wargames revealed that organic anti-tank battalions were not the solution since the divisions tended to deploy them along the main-line-of-

The performance of the tank destroyer battalions in North Africa was controversial. This column of M3 75mm GMCs was knocked out during the fighting around Kasserine Pass in February 1943. (NARA)

resistance, and not maintain them in a reserve to respond to armored attack. As a result, when the enemy tanks suddenly appeared, it was difficult to extract the anti-tank guns from their position, move them to the threatened sector and redeploy them in time to repel the enemy tank attack. What was needed was a vital mass of anti-tank weapons under a centralized control that could be dispatched when the panzer threat was identified. The use of separate anti-tank battalions assigned at corps level seemed the best solution. There was some debate as to which combat arm would be responsible for the new weapons. The anti-tank concept was largely the brainchild of the artillery branch, but the War Department decided that it should be managed by a new command, which could devote its full attention to the problem. As a result, the Tank Destroyer Center was established at Ft. Hood, Texas, in December 1941, headed by Gen. Andrew D. Bruce, an officer from the planning branch of the War Department G-3 office who had been in charge of the tank destroyer project since 1940. On December 3, all anti-tank battalions were removed from the divisions, renamed as tank destroyer battalions, and placed under GHQ control. The change in name of the battalions was supposed to symbolize the change in tactics from defensive to offensive.

Bruce had been pushing for some time for a more dynamic response to the tank threat than the artillery branch's approach, which continued to favor towed guns. The new motto of the tank destroyers—"Seek, Strike, Destroy"—emphasized the view that speed and mobility were key. The tank destroyers would remain behind the front lines in reserve, and when the panzer attack became evident, they would rush to the scene at high speed and destroy the panzers in a fast-moving battle of maneuver.

Tables of organization and equipment were approved on December 24, 1941, for two types of tank destroyer battalions—light and heavy. The light tank destroyer battalion had three companies each with 12 towed or self-propelled 37mm anti-tank guns, for a total of 36 per battalion. The heavy tank destroyer battalion had three companies each with four self-propelled 37mm anti-tank guns and eight self-propelled 3in. anti-tank guns. There was a surge of organization in December 1941 as 53 tank destroyer battalions were created consisting of 26 towed light battalions, two self-propelled light battalions, and 25 heavy battalions. The heavy battalions were often created from existing divisional anti-tank battalions. The large number of light towed battalions was a tacit recognition that better equipment was not yet available.

The issue of what type of weapons were ultimately needed for the tank destroyers was a long-running controversy within the army, and a source of rancorous debate between Gens. McNair and Bruce. McNair was an artilleryman and favored the use of towed guns as a more economical solution to the tank problem; Bruce felt that towed guns were too slow to deploy and favored self-propelled weapons. The Armored Force weighed in and suggested that they use tanks. Bruce retorted that he wanted something faster and lighter than tanks, more akin to "a cruiser than a battleship." The tank destroyer advocates fixed on a legend from the 1940 campaign that the French army had successfully used anti-tank guns mounted in the rear of trucks to defeat the panzers and saw this as a short-term technical solution to their problem. The first US Army tank destroyers were expedient designs, rushed into production to equip the weaponless new battalions. The French 75mm gun was bolted into the back of the M3 halftrack, resulting in the M3 75mm gun motor carriage (GMC), while the new 37mm anti-tank gun was placed on a pedestal mount in the rear of the Dodge 2¹/₂-ton truck to result in the M6 37mm GMC light tank destroyer. A more satisfactory design appeared in June 1942 as the M10 3in. GMC consisting of a 3in. gun mounted in an open turret on the M4A2 medium tank chassis but with lighter armor than the basic tank version. Gen. Bruce opposed the production of the M10 tank destroyer as being simply another expedient design without the speed and agility he desired in a tank destroyer.

He was overruled by the army bureaucracy, which wanted an adequate design in production as quickly as possible to equip the many new battalions. From March to August 1942, 27 more tank destroyer battalions had been formed, bringing the total to 80, and there was a desperate need for a modern weapon for these units. The first M10 3in. GMC was completed in September 1942 and they were quickly put into service.

The tank destroyer force endured considerable organizational turmoil in 1942 and 1943 due to the erratic supply of new equipment and changing ideas about their organization. As the M6 37mm GMC became available, the towed tank destroyer battalions were gradually converted to self-propelled battalions, and a refined TO&E for these light battalions was issued on June 8, 1942. The first tank destroyers were deployed to the Philippines in December 1941, but they were neither trained nor organized as tank destroyers. Fifty M3 75mm GMC were used to form three battalions of the Provisional Field Artillery Brigade, which was part of the Provisional Tank Group. The first deployment of actual tank destroyer battalions took place in November 1942 for Operation Torch in North Africa. The 601st Tank Destroyer Battalion was landed in November 1942, still organized as a composite heavy battalion with a mixture of M6 37mm GMC and M3 75mm GMC. Two more battalions followed in December 1942, and four in January 1943. Two of these, the 776th and 805th TD Battalions, were the first in combat with the new M10 3in. GMC. The M10 saw its combat debut with the 805th TD Battalion at El Guettar on March 23, 1943. The fighting at El Guettar was the sole example of the tank destroyer battalions being used according to doctrine as a concentrated force to repulse a massed tank attack. The attack was staged by the 10th Panzer Division with about 50 tanks and the 601st and 899th Tank Destroyer Battalions helped beat it off, claiming to have knocked out about 30 German tanks in the process. However, the 601st lost 20 of its 28 M3 75mm GMC and the 899th lost seven M10 3in. GMC. There was considerably less tank fighting in the later stage of the campaign and the tank destroyers were sometimes used as expedient field artillery, a role that they would also adopt in Italy in 1943–44.

The lessons from tank destroyer combat in North Africa were a source of controversy within the army's senior ranks with factions seeing the campaign as vindicating their own point of view. Gen. Bruce pointed to the battle at El Guettar as a shining example of the potential of tank destroyers. Other officers pointed out that tank destroyers had completely failed to stop the German tank attacks at Sidi-bou-Zid and Kasserine Pass, that the one engagement at El Guettar was a Pyrrhic victory with tank destroyer losses as high as panzer losses, and that the tank destroyers in North Africa had little to show even though they numbered ten battalions. Maj. Gen. John Lucas, a special observer for the army chief-of-staff, concluded that "the Tank Destroyer has, in my opinion, failed to prove its usefulness ... I believe that the doctrine of an offensive weapon to 'slug it out' with the tank is unsound." Lucas supported the deployment of purely defensive anti-tank weapons such as anti-tank guns. Armored Force chief Lt. Gen. Jacob Devers toured North Africa and concluded, "the separate tank destroyer arm is not a practical concept on the battlefield. Defensive anti-tank weapons are essentially artillery. Offensively, the best way to beat the tank is a better tank." Senior commanders in Tunisia, including George Patton and Omar Bradley, were unhappy with the performance of the offensively oriented tank destroyer units, finding them unsuited to actual battlefield conditions.

The most pernicious effect of the North African controversy was that it gave free rein to Gen. McNair to pander to the long-standing prejudices of his fellow artillerymen in favor of towed anti-tank guns. McNair pointed to the successes of British towed anti-tank guns in the fighting in the autumn of 1942 at El Alamein as vindication of the towed anti-tank gun concept. McNair's argument confused a technical issue with a tactical issue. The British anti-tank guns had been effective at El Alamein because the British had been prudent enough to deploy the more powerful 6-pdr. (57mm) anti-tank gun in a timely fashion while the US Army had clung to the obsolete and ineffective 37mm anti-tank gun in its divisional anti-tank companies. The British example did not answer the tactical dilemma of whether it made sense any longer to deploy specialized defensive anti-tank battalions when the US Army was about to embark on a series of campaigns that were primarily offensive in nature.

McNair's assessment of the lessons of the North African campaign was a collection of ex post facto excuses for policies he had been pursuing before El Alamein. In August 1942, McNair pushed for the manufacture of a towed version of the 3in. gun currently used on the M10 3in. GMC even though Gen. Bruce vigorously opposed it. On August 22, 1942, McNair ordered the Tank Destroyer Center to restudy the issue of towed anti-tank guns, noting that they could be unloaded at ports that could not handle heavy tracked vehicles. Gen. Bruce argued that a towed battalion required 300 more men than a self-propelled battalion and required more shipping space since it involved not only the towed gun but its prime mover as well. On January 1, 1943, McNair ordered Bruce to create and test a towed battalion and the 801st Tank Destroyer Battalion served as the guinea pig. The trials resulted in a tentative organization and on March 31, 1943, McNair ordered the conversion of 15 self-propelled battalions into towed battalions. To keep the battalion size down, the reconnaissance company was eliminated in towed battalions, which only had a much smaller reconnaissance platoon in the HQ company. In November 1943, McNair ordered that half of all tank destroyer battalions would be converted to towed configuration in time for the forthcoming

In practice, tank destroyer tactics in the ETO bore little resemblance to doctrine and were more similar to those employed by the separate tank battalions for infantry support. M10 tank destroyers of the 818th TD Battalion support infantry of the 5th Infantry Division near Fountainebleu on August 23, 1944. (NARA)

campaign in France. During the autumn 1943 Louisiana wargames, the newly converted 823rd Tank Destroyer Battalion was attached to several different divisions to show them the uses and limitations of the new formation. As would become evident in the campaign in France, McNair's decision to shift the tank destroyer battalions to a towed configuration made a mediocre combat formation even worse.

If this was not bad enough, Gen. Bruce's actions in the technical realm did little to improve the prospects for the successful combat use of the tank destroyer battalions in 1944. Bruce had been pushing for a new self-propelled tank destroyer design since 1941, placing a great deal of emphasis on the need for high speed. Bruce was so adamant on this point that the head of the Special Armored Board, Brig. Gen. W. B. Palmer, complained that his exorbitant expectations would prevent a vehicle from being ready in time to participate in the 1944 campaigns. Bruce finally settled on the new M18 76mm GMC as being the answer to his prayers. While the M18 was much faster than the M10, it was also more weakly armored and was so small that its fighting compartment was not as efficient as the M10's in combat conditions. The firepower of both vehicles was essentially the same, so many officers questioned whether the M18 was justified. Gen. Omar Bradley refused to have the type deployed with his First US Army after trial deployments at Anzio in February 1944 received very mixed reviews. Bruce had let his obsession with high mobility distract him from the primary mission of the tank destroyer force, namely the ability to destroy enemy tanks. When the Ordnance tried to win support for mounting the 90mm gun on the M10 in anticipation of German armor improvements, Bruce objected, arguing that it was not fast

The towed tank destroyers were sometimes used for cordon defense. Here, a 3in. anti-tank gun of the 823rd Tank Destroyer Battalion supports the 117th Infantry, 30th Division, during the fighting in Schauffenburg, Germany, on October 9. The day before, Panzer Brigade 108 had attacked the regiment but was beaten off by US tanks. (NARA)

enough. As a result, when US Army tank destroyer battalions were deployed in France in 1944, they were still equipped with the same 3in. tank destroyers available since 1942, and worse yet, many were the cumbersome new towed guns. No thanks to Bruce or McNair, Ordnance succeeded in getting the more powerful M36 90mm GMC into limited production by the subterfuge that it would be needed later in 1944 to deal with Siegfried Line bunkers.

This string of unfortunate decisions undermined the ability of the US Army to deal with the German panzer threat in France in 1944. US doctrine put undue emphasis on the use of tank destroyers to deal with the tank threat, even after the Tunisian campaign raised real questions about the viability of the doctrine. When the Armored Force under Gen. Devers tried to push for better tank guns to deal with the future panzer threat in 1943, they were rebuffed by the AGF, which argued that it ran counter to army doctrine that assigned tank destroyers the primary role for this mission. At the same time, the combination of tactical mistakes by the AGF in insisting on the deployment of ineffective towed tank destroyer battalions, combined with the Tank Destroyer Center's inept direction of the technical development of anti-tank weapons, further undermined the already dubious tank destroyer doctrine.

These trends were symptomatic of a broader failure within the US Army to anticipate the evolution of the panzers beyond those encountered in North Africa and Italy. While US tanks and tank destroyers were capable of dealing with the mainstay of the panzer force in 1942–43, the PzKpfw IV, they were unprepared to deal with its successor, the Panther tank, which made up about half the panzer force in France in June 1944. In addition, US Army anti-tank doctrine was undermined by a failure to appreciate the changes in the nature of panzer operations since the seminal 1940 campaign in France. The Wehrmacht in France in 1940 concentrated its tanks in a dozen panzer divisions. As Wehrmacht combined-arms doctrine evolved in 1941–44, mechanization deepened. By 1944, the armored vehicle had become ubiquitous on the battlefield not only in the form of tanks, but as heavily armored assault guns such as the StuG III and tank destroyers such as the Jagdpanzer IV. Instead of panzers being encountered in concentrated masses, German armored vehicles were encountered daily almost all over the battlefield, whether in panzer divisions, infantry support units, or in specialized panzer formations such as tank destroyer and heavy tank battalions. Concentrated tank destroyer battalions were a poor antidote to such a dispersed threat.

Preparation for war

The tank battalions

The separate tank battalions were raised and trained at over 20 different army bases across the United States. By far the most important were Ft. Knox, Ft. Benning, Ft. Lewis, Camp Campbell, and Camp Bowie, which between them accounted for more than half of the separate tank battalions raised in 1941–43. In some cases, the bases included a Tank Group or Armored Group headquarters, which helped to manage the training process. Specialized tank crew training and officer training was conducted at the Armored Forces schools at Ft. Knox, Kentucky. Not all tank crews received training at Ft. Knox. Generally, a portion of the tankers in any particular battalion would be trained at Ft. Knox to serve as the cadre for a battalion, and then this training would be passed along to other troops of the battalion at their home base. Another approach was to have a trained tank battalion or armored division provide a portion of their trained personnel to form the basis for a new tank battalion, who in turn trained the new troops.

In general, US Army standards for technical training of tank crews in issues such as tank operation, tank gunnery, tank maintenance and related skills were at a high standard in most battalions deployed to the ETO in 1944–45. There was ample opportunity since many of these units were formed one or more years before their combat deployment. The US Army paid close attention to British training practices for tank crews to learn of any improvements which might be incorporated into the US training program due to greater British experience. Assessments after Tunisia concluded that overall, the existing training programs were adequate except in some specific areas.

Training in tank–infantry cooperation was very spotty, especially prior to the autumn of 1943, and some tank battalions received little or no significant training with infantry units stateside prior to the summer of 1944. This was a particular source of criticism by army observers in Tunisia and Sicily. The focus was not only on the problems at small unit level, but also on the unpreparedness of senior infantry commanders to properly employ tank units in conjunction with infantry divisions. The AGF changes in the spring of 1944 did not have as much impact on units already deployed to the UK in preparation for the invasion as it did on stateside units. In part this was due to time lag between AGF directives and action in the field, but there were also problems in conducting exercises in Britain in the spring of 1944 due to the congestion of all the US units being funneled into the UK for the invasion. In addition, training was often unrealistic. The US Army in 1943–44 did not have a great deal of practical experience in fighting of the type that would be encountered in Europe in 1944–45. Lessons from the Italian campaign were slow in making their way through the system and were not entirely applicable to the situations that would arise in France.

Tactical doctrine was standardized by means of Field Manuals (FM), which reflected current army thinking on the best approaches to standard combat situations. The basic tactical manual for junior battalion leaders was *FM 17–32: The Tank Company*, which was first approved on August 2, 1942. This manual was common between the tank battalions of armored divisions and those of the separate tank battalions and covered basic issues such as basic concepts of organization and employment; unit communication; marches, bivouacs, and security; offensive and defensive combat; supply, evacuation, and casualty evacuation. The corresponding manual for the senior battalion leaders was *FM 17–33: The Armored Battalion, Light and Medium* approved on September 18, 1942. This covered many of the same issues as the company manual, but provided more depth. In both cases, a team of tank officers on active duty in Italy prepared a revised edition and these were released in November 1944.

One of the most important training aids was the new *FM 17–36: Employment of Tanks With Infantry*, and a tentative edition was released in March 1944 shortly before the start of the campaign in France. The two previous field manuals pre-dated early US combat experience in Tunisia and Italy, while the new *FM 17–36* was able to provide more practical advice on the conduct of

Some tank battalions were rotated through the Desert Training Center in the Mojave Desert of southern California for large-scale exercises. (NARA)

tank operations. After all the misunderstandings about the role of tanks in operations with infantry, the new field manual explicitly described their missions, and laid out what was expected of the tanks and what was expected of the infantry in joint operations. The tanks were expected to neutralize or destroy enemy automatic weapons holding up the infantry; neutralize an objective until the arrival of the infantry; neutralize hostile reserves and artillery; destroy or disrupt enemy command, communication, and supply installations; break up counterattacks; support infantry with fire; and make paths through wire and similar obstacles. The infantry was expected to seize ground suitable for the tanks to launch a further attack; destroy or neutralize enemy anti-tank weapons; closely follow the tank attack to assist by fire, seize the objectives, mop-up, and protect reorganization of the tanks; protect the tanks from enemy infantry anti-tank efforts, especially in close terrain such as towns and wooded areas; provide a base of fire for the tank attack; and remove obstacles, especially mines, that were holding up a tank attack. A supplement to this field manual was issued on July 7, 1944, which provided specific tactical problems and proposed solutions to these problems.

The tank destroyer battalions

The training and preparation of the tank destroyer battalions followed much the same pattern as the tank battalions. The battalions were raised at many bases across the United States, with the tank destroyer groups playing a role in training the units. The primary specialist training post for tank destroyer personnel was Ft. Hood, Texas, the headquarters for the Tank Destroyer Center. Besides its role for specialist training, Ft. Hood was also the location where the largest number of battalions was raised, at one point reaching 28 battalions and eight tank destroyer groups.

The fundamentals of tank destroyer doctrine were laid out in *FM 18–5: Organization and Tactics of Tank Destroyer Units*, which was approved on June 16, 1942. The field manual stressed "tank destroyer units are especially designed for offensive action against armored forces. They are capable of semi-independent

A 3in. gun of the 614th Tank Destroyer Battalion is seen during training in France in September 1944. The US Army was still segregated in World War II, and two African-American tank destroyer battalions saw combat in France in 1944–45. (NARA)

action, but preferably operate in close cooperation with friendly units of all arms." The manual also reiterated the important tactical concept that during defensive actions, tank destroyer units were not primarily to be used for forward defense of the main-line-of-resistance, but rather kept in mobile reserve to respond to enemy tank attacks. The field manual suggested that the usual distribution of the tank destroyer battalions would be on a scale of one battalion per armored or infantry division, one or more tank destroyer groups with each corps, and a similar allotment of groups at the army level for independent assignments. The manual emphasized the offensive orientation of the battalion, and noted that for individual tank destroyers, offensive action "consists of vigorous reconnaissance to locate hostile tanks and movement to advantageous positions from which to attack the enemy by fire. Tank destroyers avoid 'slugging matches' with tanks, but compensate for their light armor and difficulty of concealment by exploitation of their mobility and superior observation."

The attempted use of this doctrine in Tunisia in 1942 proved to be a complete failure from the perspective of the AGF, and led to a swift set of instructions that a new tactical doctrine had to be developed. In addition, there was widespread dissatisfaction with the training at Ft. Hood, which tended to emphasize technical training at the expense of discipline. This came under vociferous criticism from the army chief-of-staff, Gen. George C. Marshall, who encountered one of the battalions while attending the Casablanca conference in January 1943. Training of several of the battalions sent to North Africa had been rushed, and the lack of preparation was plainly evident to many senior commanders.

In the wake of the North African campaign, the Tank Destroyer Center attempted to quell the widespread criticism of tank destroyer performance by instituting training changes as well as formulating new doctrine. There was considerable turmoil in late 1943 as numerous self-propelled battalions were reorganized into towed battalions at the insistence of Gen. McNair. It became quickly apparent that the new battalions needed fundamentally different training, since a towed gun had substantially different tactical and technical requirements from the more tank-like self-propelled tank destroyers. Another change instituted in 1943 on the basis of experiences in North Africa and Italy was to add secondary training in indirect artillery fire to the program. Many tank destroyer officers came from the artillery branch, but this added an additional training burden on the force.

The poor performance of the tank destroyers in Tunisia led to plans to trim back the size of the force. Initial plans in 1941 had called for as many as 220 battalions, reduced to 144 in 1943, and further trimmed back to 106 by the end of 1943. Of the 106 battalions, 61 were shipped to Europe and ten to the Pacific theater, leaving 35 in the United States with little demand for their services. The AGF decided that these were surplus, and in October 1943 began making plans to disband them for their personnel or convert them to other roles such as field artillery, tank, or amphibious tractor battalions. The first five were converted in December 1943, and most of the remainder in March–May 1944.

The Tank Destroyer Center had completed a new edition of the basic *FM 18–5* field manual in May 1943, but the AGF was so unhappy with it that many revisions were demanded. As a result, it was not re-issued until July 1944, by which time many tank destroyer battalions had already been posted to the ETO. In recognition of the fact that the towed battalions would have to fight in a fundamentally different fashion from the self-propelled battalions, two different platoon manuals were issued alongside, *FM 18–20* for the self-propelled battalions, and *FM 18–21* for the towed battalions. The impact of these new manuals is open to question, as by the time they were issued, the majority of the battalions were already overseas and learning first hand that their training and doctrine was unrealistic in actual combat situations.

Unit organization

Six of the tank battalions deployed in the ETO in the summer of 1944 were equipped with the Leaflet tank, a top-secret night-fighting tank with a searchlight turret in place of the usual 37mm gun turret found on the basic M3A1 medium tank. Although never used as intended, some Leaflet tanks saw combat in the spring of 1945 guarding the key Rhine River crossings. (Patton Museum)

The tank battalion

The separate tank battalions that entered combat in June 1944 in the ETO were primarily based on TO&E 17–25 from September 15, 1943. An amendment on October 2, 1943, authorized the use of a medium tank for the artillery observer and there were small modifications on October 27 and November 8, 1943, and February 12, 1944. These changes were incorporated in a new table on November 18, 1944, (which is shown in more detail in Battle Orders 3: *US Armored Divisions: The European Theater of Operations, 1944–45* by the same author, Osprey: Oxford, 2004).

The separate tank battalions had six companies: a headquarters and HQ company; a service company; three medium tank companies (lettered A through C) and a light tank company (company D). The battalion HQ section traveled by jeep and halftrack, and there were two tanks for the battalion commander and the executive officer. Besides its support sections, the HQ company had a recon platoon relying primarily on "bantams," the 1/4-ton truck more commonly called jeeps elsewhere in the army. In addition, there was an 81mm mortar platoon, and an assault-gun platoon consisting of three M4 105mm assault guns. The M4 assault gun was essentially similar to a normal M4 tank, but was fitted with a 105mm howitzer instead of the usual 75mm gun. The battalion's service company contained a maintenance platoon and a supply and transportation platoon. The

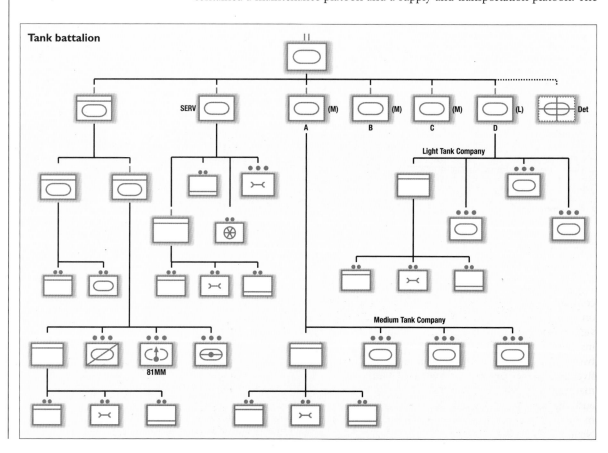

maintenance platoon was responsible for battlefield recovery of damaged tanks as well as unit-level maintenance and repair. The supply and transportation platoon, as its name implies, was responsible for transporting and delivering the battalion's food, fuel, ammunition, and other essentials and the 2$\frac{1}{2}$-ton truck was the backbone of this unit.

The combat elements of the battalion were the four tank companies. Each company was designed to be moderately self-sufficient for short durations, and each had its own maintenance and administrative, mess and supply section which was primarily used for providing food to the unit.

Tank battalion table of organization and equipment						
TO&E 17–25 September 15, 1943	HQ & HQ company	Medium tank company (x 3)	Light tank company	Service company	Medical detachment	Total
Officers	13	5	5	4	2	39
Enlisted men	134	117	92	112	20	709
.45-cal. pistol	3	0	0	0	0	3
.45-cal. SMG	47	95	73	44	0	449
.30-cal. carbine	77	27	24	75	0	257
.30-cal. M1 rifle	20	0	0	0	0	20
.30-cal. LMG	3	1	1	11	0	18
.50-cal. M2 HMG	5	1	2	10	0	20
2.36in. bazooka	12	3	2	12	0	35
81mm mortar	0	1	1	2	0	6
M5A1 light tank	0	0	17	0	0	17
M4 medium tank	2	17	0	0	0	53
M4 (105mm)	3	1	0	0	0	6
M32 TRV	0	1	1	2	0	6
Halftrack	8	1	1	1	2	15
$\frac{1}{4}$-ton jeep	11	2	2	3	1	23
$\frac{3}{4}$-ton ambulance	0	0	0	0	1	1
$\frac{3}{4}$-ton WC truck	0	0	0	2	2	4
2$\frac{1}{2}$-ton truck	1	1	1	34	0	39
Heavy wrecking truck	0	0	0	2	0	2
M10 ammo trailer	4	0	0	13	0	17
$\frac{1}{4}$-ton trailer	11	2	2	3	4	26
1-ton trailer	2	1	1	20	1	27

As mentioned earlier, two tank battalions in the ETO remained in a light tank configuration. These battalions were smaller than a normal tank battalion with only three tank companies instead of four. There was no suitable tank recovery vehicle for the light tank battalions, so M5A1 light tanks were authorized instead. An amendment was released on June 21, 1944, that deleted the two halftracks used as ambulances in the medical detachment, and substituted five light tank recovery vehicles (TRV) for the five light tanks used in the maintenance role. In fact light TRVs were never manufactured and the authorized substitute was either a light tank as before, or more commonly a M32 medium TRV. Another modified table with minor modifications was released on November 11, 1944.

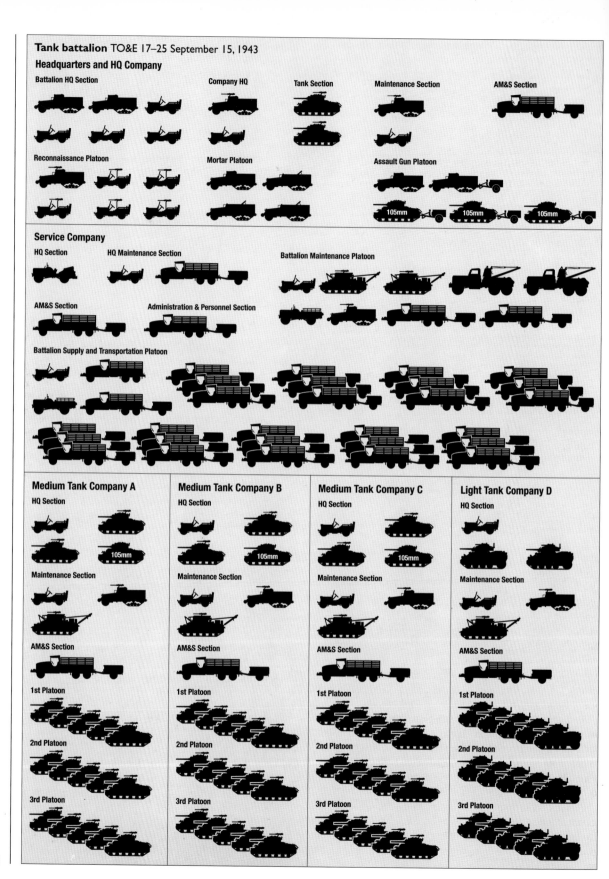

Tank battalion TO&E 17–25 September 15, 1943

Headquarters and HQ Company

Battalion HQ Section

Company HQ

Tank Section

Maintenance Section

AM&S Section

Reconnaissance Platoon

Mortar Platoon

Assault Gun Platoon

105mm 105mm 105mm

Service Company

HQ Section

HQ Maintenance Section

Battalion Maintenance Platoon

AM&S Section

Administration & Personnel Section

Battalion Supply and Transportation Platoon

Medium Tank Company A

HQ Section

105mm

Maintenance Section

AM&S Section

1st Platoon

2nd Platoon

3rd Platoon

Medium Tank Company B

HQ Section

105mm

Maintenance Section

AM&S Section

1st Platoon

2nd Platoon

3rd Platoon

Medium Tank Company C

HQ Section

105mm

Maintenance Section

AM&S Section

1st Platoon

2nd Platoon

3rd Platoon

Light Tank Company D

HQ Section

Maintenance Section

AM&S Section

1st Platoon

2nd Platoon

3rd Platoon

TO&E 17–15 November 12, 1943	HQ & HQ company	Light tank company (x 3)	Service company	Medical detachment	Total
Officers	13	5	4	2	34
Enlisted men	131	92	91	15	513
.45-cal. pistol	3	0	0	0	3
.45-cal. SMG	45	73	29	0	293
.30-cal. carbine	76	24	69	0	217
.30-cal. M1 rifle	20	0	0	0	20
.50-cal. M2 HMG	5	2	6	0	17
2.36in. bazooka	12	1	7	0	22
M5A1 light tank	3	18	2	0	59
M8 75mm HMC	3	0	0	0	3
M21 81mm MMC	3	0	0	0	3
Halftrack	8	1	2	0	13
1/4-ton jeep	11	2	3	1	21
3/4-ton ambulance	0	0	0	1	1
3/4-ton WC truck	0	0	2	1	3
2 1/2-ton truck	1	1	19	0	23
Heavy wrecking truck	0	0	2	0	2
M10 ammo trailer	4	0	6	0	10
1/4-ton trailer	11	2	3	4	24
1-ton trailer	2	1	12	0	17

Light tank battalion table of organization and equipment

The most secret of the US separate tank battalions were those formed under Project Cassock in 1943. In 1942, the British Army revealed that it was working on a concept for night-fighting tanks that were given the cover name "Canal Defence Light" (CDL). A formation of CDL tanks would illuminate the battlefield with intense beams of light, blinding the German defenders while making the enemy positions evident to the attacking force. In November 1942, the US Army joined the British program and built CDL tanks in the US. There was a clear understanding between the British and American sides that the US would not use the CDL tanks without coordinating the operation with British officials first, since it was presumed that the CDL tanks would be most effective as a surprise weapon for a particularly important mission. The American CDL tanks were given the cover name of T10 Shop Tractors but were codenamed "Leaflet" for operational use.

To maintain secrecy, the Leaflet tanks were deployed only with the 9th and 10th Armored Groups. Six battalions were formed in 1943: the 701st, 736th, 738th, 739th, 740th, and 748th Tank Battalions (Special), and were trained at Camp Bouse in the remote Arizona desert to preserve the intense secrecy of the project.

Each special platoon had five Leaflet tanks and an accompanying M4 medium tank. The tactics were for the Leaflet tanks to advance in a line with each tank spaced about 25 yards apart. The M4 "fighter" tank was intended to provide security for the platoon as

The US Army was still segregated in World War II, and two African-American tank battalions, the 761st and 784th, saw combat in the ETO. This is an M5A1 light tank of Co. D, 761st Tank Battalion, in Germany in 1945. (NARA)

Light tank battalion TO&E 17–15 November 12, 1943

Headquarters and HQ Company

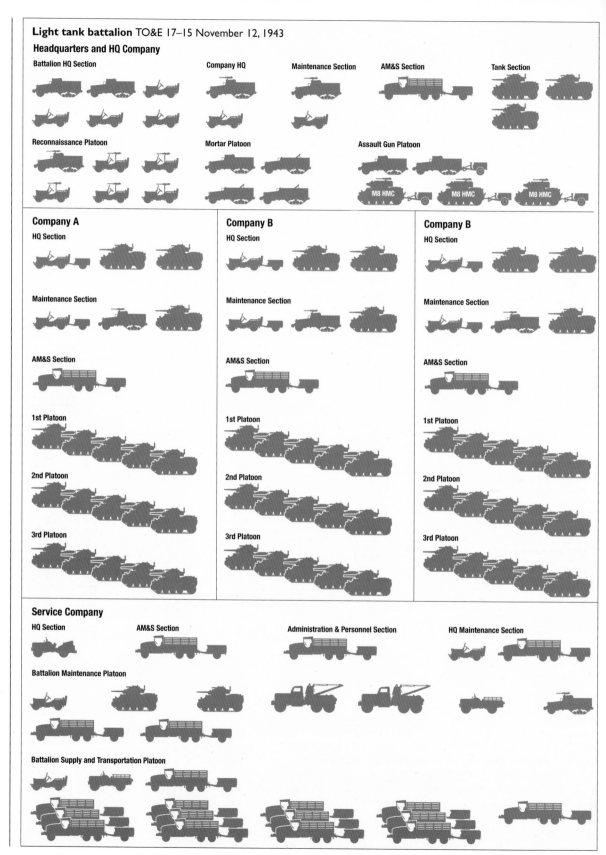

Battalion HQ Section

Company HQ

Maintenance Section

AM&S Section

Tank Section

Reconnaissance Platoon

Mortar Platoon

Assault Gun Platoon

M8 HMC · M8 HMC · M8 HMC

Company A

HQ Section

Maintenance Section

AM&S Section

1st Platoon

2nd Platoon

3rd Platoon

Company B

HQ Section

Maintenance Section

AM&S Section

1st Platoon

2nd Platoon

3rd Platoon

Company B

HQ Section

Maintenance Section

AM&S Section

1st Platoon

2nd Platoon

3rd Platoon

Service Company

HQ Section

AM&S Section

Administration & Personnel Section

HQ Maintenance Section

Battalion Maintenance Platoon

Battalion Supply and Transportation Platoon

well as to engage targets of opportunity. The Leaflet tanks retained their 75mm hull gun and so could also engage targets.

In the event, the special battalions were so secret that senior Allied commanders never incorporated them into any of their plans. In the autumn of 1944, the commander of the US 10th Armored Group visited a number of army and corps commanders attempting to interest them in their combat value. However, no troops had been trained to operate with the battalions, and many commanders were skeptical of their value. There was such a shortage of normal tank battalions at the time that on November 4, 1944, Eisenhower's headquarters decided to put the Leaflet tanks in mothballs and to begin converting four of the battalions into normal tank battalions, and the other two into the new "Tank Battalion (Special-Mine Exploder/SMX)" equipped with flail tanks and mine rollers. As a result, none of the special tank battalions was ever committed to combat as intended.

Tank battalion (special) table of organization and equipment					
TO&E 17–45S December 4, 1943	HQ & HQ company	Medium tank company (x 3)	Service company	Medical detachment	Total
Officers	11	5	7	2	35
Enlisted men	94	147	114	20	669
.45-cal. pistol	3	0	0	0	3
.45-cal. SMG	34	120	45	0	439
.30-cal. carbine	50	32	76	0	222
.30-cal. M1 rifle	18	0	0	0	18
.50-cal. M2 HMG	3	2	11	0	20
2.36in. bazooka	6	3	12	0	27
M4 medium tank	3	5	0	0	18
Leaflet tank	0	18	0	0	54
Halftrack	5	1	1	3	12
M32 TRV	0	1	2	0	5
1/4-ton jeep	14	2	3	1	24
3/4-ton truck	1	0	2	1	4
2 1/2-ton truck	1	1	35	0	39
Heavy wrecking truck	0	0	2	0	2
M10 ammo trailer	0	0	14	0	14
1-ton trailer	2	1	21	0	26

The US Army considered forming special airborne tank units after the successful use of German paratroops at Eben Emael in 1940 and Crete in 1941. With the development of the T9 airborne tank underway, in February 1943, the AGF ordered the Armored Force to organize an airborne tank battalion and develop suitable training and doctrine in cooperation with the Airborne Command. However, the Airborne Command was skeptical about the need for a battalion-sized formation due to the airlift problem, so the first unit was trimmed down to a company. The 151st Airborne Tank Company was activated at Ft. Knox on August 15, 1943, followed by the 28th Airborne Tank Battalion on December 6, 1943. In spite of considerable enthusiasm within the army for the concept, the Marmon Herrington T9 airborne tank proved to be so

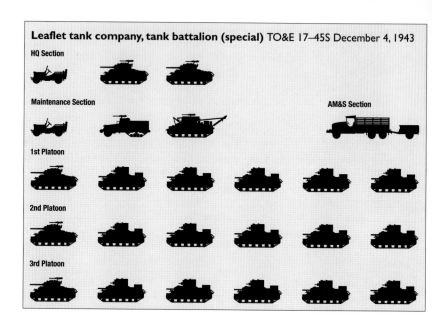

Leaflet tank company, tank battalion (special) TO&E 17–45S December 4, 1943

HQ Section

Maintenance Section

AM&S Section

1st Platoon

2nd Platoon

3rd Platoon

disappointing from a technical standpoint, that enthusiasm soon waned. The 151st Airborne Tank Company was not available in time for deployment with airborne units on D-Day, and in July 1944 was transferred from Ft. Knox to Camp Mackall, North Carolina, where it was quickly forgotten. The 28th Airborne Tank Battalion was reorganized as a conventional tank battalion in October 1944. The T9E1 airborne tank was finally accepted for service as the M22 airborne tank, and apparently a small number were sent to the 6th Army Group in 1944 in Alsace for potential use. However, no airborne tank unit was deployed in combat during the war.

The battalion was lighter than a conventional light tank battalion, having no service company and very few supporting vehicles. It was presumed that the unit would be used on short-duration missions and that the battalion could be supported at least in part by the airborne divisions it was supporting.

The 28th Tank Battalion (Airborne) was the only unit of its kind formed during the war, but it was not deployed into combat with its M22 light airborne tanks. (Patton Museum)

TO&E 17–55 January 15, 1944	HQ & HQ company	Airborne tank company (x 3)	Enlisted cadre	Medical detachment	Total
Officers	11	5	0	1	27
Enlisted men	128	72	109	12	465
.45-cal. pistol	3	0	0	0	3
.45-cal. SMG	40	57	0	0	211
.30-cal. carbine	84	20	0	0	144
.30-cal. LMG	16	2	0	0	22
.50-cal. M2 HMG	17	2	0	0	23
2.36in. bazooka	5	1	0	0	8
M22 airborne tank	2	18	0	0	56
75mm pack howitzer	3	0	0	0	3
1/4-ton jeep	26	4	0	3	41
3/4-ton WC truck	10	1	0	0	13
1/4-ton trailer	17	4	0	3	32

Airborne tank battalion table of organization and equipment

Separate tank battalion equipment

Officially, there was no difference in equipment between the separate tank battalions and the tank battalions belonging to the armored divisions although in practice the armored divisions often received priority for new tank types. At the beginning of the campaign in the ETO in Normandy in June 1944, the principal tank of the separate tank battalions was the M4 medium tank. The M4 and M4A1 were used interchangeably in the battalions and were in fact identical except that the M4 used a welded hull and the M4A1 used a cast hull. The army had established a preference for the M4A3 with the new Ford GAA engine, but these did not begin to appear in the ETO until August 1944 with the arrival of battalions more recently formed in the US.

The 759th Tank Battalion was one of only two battalions in the ETO to retain the dubious light tank battalion configuration. They were entirely equipped with the obsolete M5A1 light tank and some tanks of Company B are seen in Montebourg, France, in June 1944 (MHI)

The 75mm gun versions of the Sherman tank were gradually replaced with the 76mm versions like this M4A3(76) of the 709th Tank Battalion supporting the 75th Division during fighting in the Colmar area of France on January 31, 1945. (NARA)

A new 76mm gun had been developed for the M4 series, but was not immediately accepted by the First US Army although some were available in England in April 1944. Although the new 76mm gun offered better anti-tank performance than the short 75mm gun, it had less powerful high-explosive ammunition. There was a widespread belief until Normandy that the 75mm gun was perfectly adequate to deal with the panzers, so there was considerable reluctance to lose the high-explosive firepower of the 75mm for improved but unnecessary increases in anti-tank performance. When the Panther tank was encountered in quantity in Normandy in June 1944, the opinions about the 75mm gun on the M4 dramatically changed and there was a sudden cry for better guns to deal with the Panther threat. The small inventory of M4A1 (76mm) in Britain was delivered to the 2nd and 3rd Armored Divisions in time for Operation Cobra in late July 1944. Two companies of 76mm tanks were provided to the 70th and 746th Tank Battalions on August 10. 1944, and a process gradually began of deploying these uparmed tanks as they became available. In general, there was no special deployment pattern with the new tanks. Most battalions mixed them in with the medium tank companies so that each company had a few. The 76mm tanks were deployed with the separate tank battalions a bit more slowly than with the armored divisions. As in the case of the armored divisions, the 76mm tanks did not become the predominant version in service until the last few weeks of the war.

75mm and 76mm M4 medium tanks in the separate tank battalions, 12th Army Group												
	Jun 44	Jul	Aug	Sep	Oct	Nov	Dec	Jan 45	Feb	Mar	Apr	May
75mm	245	370	650	527	508	647	525	695	733	781	669	567
76mm				95	37	166	177	259	216	305	438	607
Total	245	370	650	622	545	813	702	954	949	1086	1107	1174
76mm %	0	0	0	15.3	6.8	20.4	25.2	27.1	22.8	28.1	39.6	51.7

Data at beginning of each month

The M4A3E2 assault tank was a more heavily armored version of the basic Sherman tank and separate tank battalions had priority for the few that were available. This one is seen with the 737th Tank Battalion near Gralingen, Luxembourg, in the final phase of the Battle of the Bulge on January 22, 1945. (USAOM-APG)

The separate tank battalions received priority for only one version of the M4 medium tank, the M4A3E2 assault tank. Officers in England in 1943 recognized the need for a more heavily armored tank to eventually deal with the German Siegfried Line fortifications, and as a result, a requirement for 250 assault tanks was approved. These were similar to the normal M4A3 medium tank, but had thicker frontal and side armor, and a new, more thickly armored turret. The first batches of tanks were issued in mid-October 1944 and the separate tank battalions received priority. There was no particular deployment pattern for them so, for example, in Patton's Third Army in late November 1944, there were 15 with the 737th Tank Battalion, and five each in the 702nd, 712th, 735th and 761st Tank Battalions.

In preparation for expected river crossing operations over the Rhine, a number of tank battalions were provided with DD "Donald Duck" tanks. This is a DD tank of the 781st Tank Battalion during a practice exercise near Binau, Germany, with the floatation collar partly folded. (NARA)

The M4 (105mm) assault gun consisted of a normal M4 tank with a turret-mounted 105mm howitzer, and was used in headquarters units to provide fire support. This assault gun from the 753rd Tank Battalion is transporting infantry from the 36th Division during operations near Greisbach, Germany, on March 17, 1945. (NARA)

The M4A3E2 assault tanks were an immediate success with the tankers. In spite of their added weight, the tank crews found that the M4A3E2 assault tanks were about as maneuverable as the normal M4 medium tanks. Their main appeal, of course, was their thick armor, which was sufficient to resist direct frontal hits from the 88mm gun at typical combat ranges. Most tanks knocked out by enemy action were due to hits on the sides. On receiving an enquiry about the assault tanks from headquarters, the chief-of-staff of Patton's Third army reported, "Everyone wants the M4A3E2." In fact, the M4A3E2 proved so popular that the commander of the 6th Armored Division recommended that the Army switch to a mixture of two-thirds M4A3E2 and one-third 105mm howitzer tanks for the remainder of combat operations in 1945. However, no more M4A3E2s were forthcoming, but their success highlights the army's lack of foresight in fielding an infantry tank more suitable for use by the separate tank battalions. The War Department offered the archaic M6 heavy tank for this role in August 1944, but officers in Europe rejected this due to the excessive size and weight of this tank.

The only other major change in equipment later in the war was the arrival of the M4A3 (76mm) with 23in. tracks, also known as the M4A3E8. This introduced the new horizontal volute suspension system (HVSS), which gave the M4 tank better mobility in mud and snow. They were first deployed in late December 1944 during the Battle of the Bulge. Once again, there was no organized pattern of replacement, but in general, it would appear that armored divisions were given priority for this type. The new T26E3 tank, called the M26 Pershing after the war, was the US Army's answer to the Panther. Small numbers began to be deployed in February 1945, but these were reserved for armored divisions and saw very little combat service.

The light tank companies in the separate tank battalions were equipped with the M5A1 light tank. It was unsatisfactory as a combat vehicle in 1944, being too lightly armored and too weakly armed. A replacement tank, the M24, began arriving and saw its combat debut with the 740th Tank Battalion in the Ardennes in December 1944. Preference for these was given to the cavalry squadrons, but the type was most often seen in a few of the late-arriving armored divisions that had been reequipped in the United States in late 1944. The M24 was seldom seen in the separate tank battalions except for the 744th Tank Battalion (Light), which was completely reequipped with M24 tanks in February 1945, and the 736th Tank Battalion, which received one company in late February.

M24 light tank strength in ETO 1945					
	Jan	Feb	Mar	Apr	May
Tank battalions	20	34	67	71	97
Cavalry recon squadrons	0	12	150	302	455
Armored divisions	0	82	163	363	611
Total	20	128	380	736	1,163
Data from beginning of month					

The tank destroyer battalion

When tank destroyer battalions were first deployed in North Africa in November 1942, they were operating under the June 8, 1942, TO&E, which consisted of three companies, each with four M6 37mm GMC and 8 M3 75mm GMC. When the 37mm GMC were dropped due to their obvious obsolescence, battalions were reconstituted with 12 M10 3in. GMC in each company under the January 27, 1943, revision, so that each battalion had 36 tank destroyers. The decision to form towed battalions required an entirely separate organizational structure, so the tank destroyer battalions after May 1943 followed the existing TO&E 18–25 for the self-propelled battalions and the new TO&E 18–35 for the towed battalions. There was a revision of TO&E 18–25 in the spring of 1944, which was the standard table for the self-propelled battalions at the time of D-Day. The larger number of personnel required to man the towed guns forced the deletion of the reconnaissance company in the towed battalions, and even so the towed battalions had more troops than the self-propelled battalions.

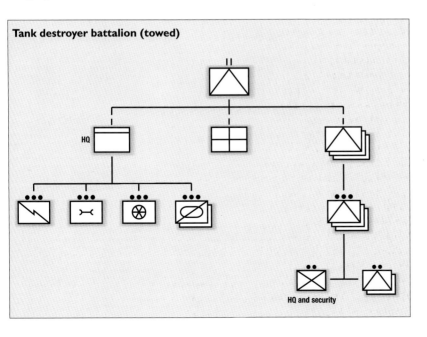

Tank destroyer battalion (towed)

HQ

HQ and security

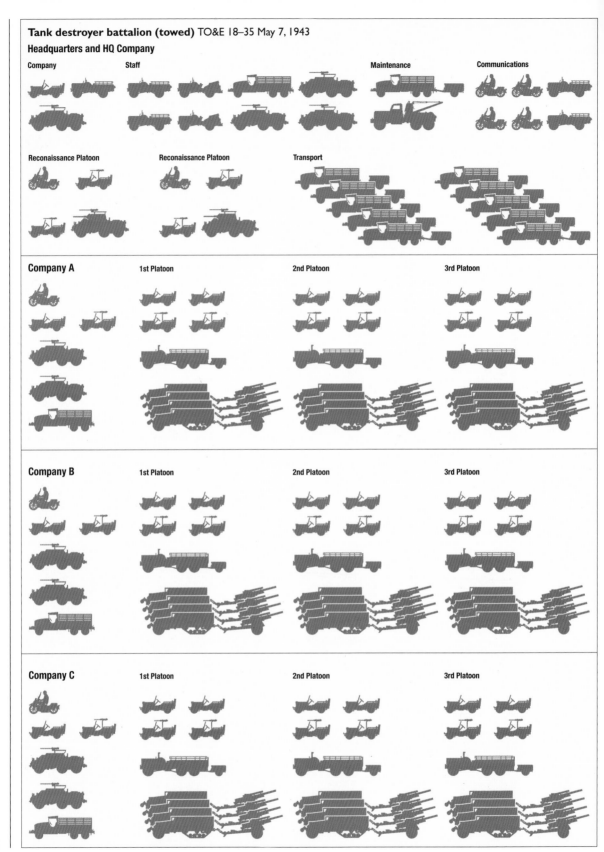

Tank destroyer battalion (towed) TO&E 18–35 May 7, 1943

Headquarters and HQ Company

Company

Staff

Maintenance

Communications

Reconaissance Platoon

Reconaissance Platoon

Transport

Company A

1st Platoon

2nd Platoon

3rd Platoon

Company B

1st Platoon

2nd Platoon

3rd Platoon

Company C

1st Platoon

2nd Platoon

3rd Platoon

Towed tank destroyer battalion table of organization and equipment

TO&E 18–35 May 7, 1943	HQ & HQ company	Tank Destroyer company (x 3)	Enlisted cadre	Medical detachment	Total
Officers	17	5	0	2	34
Enlisted men	155	197	73	17	763
.45-cal. pistol	3	0	0	0	3
.45-cal. SMG	151	49	0	0	298
.30-cal. carbine	0	120	0	0	360
.30-cal. M1 rifle	18	33	0	0	117
.30-cal. LMG	11	13	0	0	50
.50-cal. M2 HMG	4	7	0	0	25
2.36in. bazooka	26	15	0	0	71
M8 armored car	4	0	0	0	4
M20 armored car	4	2	0	0	10
M3 halftrack	0	12	0	0	36
3in. AT gun	0	12	0	0	36
Motorcycle	8	1	0	0	11
1/4-ton jeep	12	14	0	3	57
3/4-ton command	3	0	0	0	3
3/4-ton truck	5	0	0	1	6
1 1/2-ton truck	0	3	0	0	9
2 1/2-ton truck	13	1	0	0	16
Heavy wrecker	1	0	0	0	1
1/4-ton trailer	0	0	0	1	1
1-ton trailer	12	3	0	0	21

Tank destroyer battalion (self-propelled)

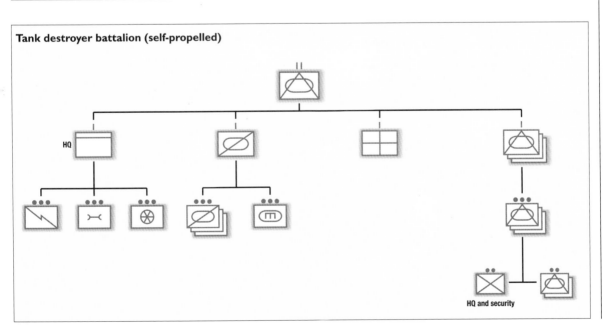

HQ

HQ and security

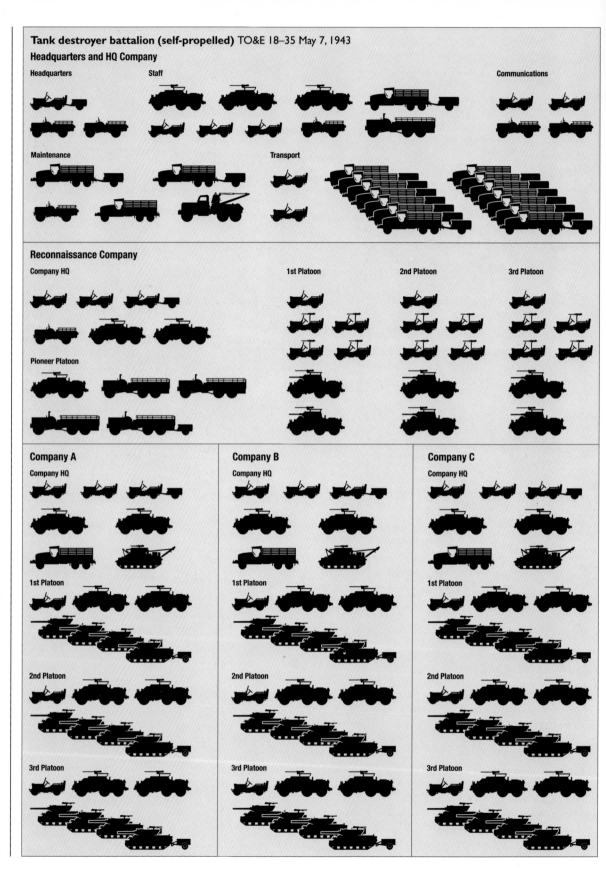

Tank destroyer battalion (self-propelled) TO&E 18–35 May 7, 1943

Headquarters and HQ Company

Headquarters   Staff   Communications

Maintenance   Transport

Reconnaissance Company

Company HQ   1st Platoon   2nd Platoon   3rd Platoon

Pioneer Platoon

Company A

Company HQ

1st Platoon

2nd Platoon

3rd Platoon

Company B

Company HQ

1st Platoon

2nd Platoon

3rd Platoon

Company C

Company HQ

1st Platoon

2nd Platoon

3rd Platoon

TO&E 18–25 March 15, 1944	HQ & HQ company	Tank Destroyer company (x 3)	Reconnaissance company	Enlisted cadre	Medical detachment	Total
Officers	13	5	6	0	1	35
Enlisted men	109	130	120	104	15	738
.45-cal. pistol	29	13	11	0	0	79
.30-cal. carbine	28	67	64	0	0	293
.30-cal. M1 rifle	67	55	51	0	0	283
.30-cal. LMG	3	5	12	0	0	30
.50-cal. M2 HMG	7	10	7	0	0	44
2.36in. bazooka	14	9	21	0	0	62
81mm mortar	0	1	0	0	0	3
M8 armored car	0	0	6	0	0	6
M20 armored car	3	8	3	0	0	30
M32 TRV	0	1	0	0	0	3
3in./76mm GMC	0	12	0	0	0	36
1/4-ton Jeep	8	6	18	0	4	48
3/4-ton truck	6	0	1	0	0	7
1 1/2-ton truck	1	0	4	0	1	6
2 1/2-ton truck	18	1	0	0	0	21
Heavy wrecker	1	0	0	0	0	1
1/4-ton trailer	1	1	2	0	0	6
M10 ammo trailer	0	3	0	0	0	9
1-ton trailer	18	0	0	0	0	18

Tank destroyer battalion equipment

At the time of D-Day, June 6, 1944, the self-propelled tank destroyer battalions were equipped with the M10 3in. GMC. This was basically a M4A2 Sherman medium tank chassis with a new superstructure with lighter armor and a new open-topped turret with a 3in. anti-tank gun. The newer M18 76mm GMC did not appear in the ETO until late July 1944, when the first M18 battalions were deployed with Patton's Third Army. It quickly became apparent that neither the M10 nor M18 was up to the task of defeating the new generation of German armored vehicles such as the Panther tank, Jagdpanzer IV tank destroyer, or Kingtiger heavy tank in frontal engagements, as their thick, well-sloped armor could not be penetrated by the 3in./76mm gun. The new-generation German panzers could only be defeated by engaging their weaker side armor. Two efforts were begun to improve this situation. A new high-velocity armor piercing (HVAP) round with a tungsten carbide core was rushed to the ETO, and first used in September 1944. While this significantly improved gun performance, tungsten carbide was not available in large quantities, and so the ammunition remained scarce for most of the campaign. The second approach was to speed up deployment of the M36 90mm GMC.

The M36 was basically an M10A1 tank destroyer with a new turret mounting a 90mm gun. They first went into action in October 1944 during the fighting along the German border. Due to the small numbers originally available, it was not possible to equip entire battalions with the M36. The initial policy was to issue it to existing M10 battalions, usually on a scale of one company at a time. As more became available, entire battalions were reequipped. The general

The 3in. anti-tank gun was towed by halftracks like the M3 halftrack seen here in St. Malo, Brittany, August 1944. (NARA)

conclusion was that the M36 was a definite improvement over the M10 when dealing with the Panther tank, though it was not the complete solution. The existing 90mm ammunition would not reliably penetrate the Panther glacis plate at ranges over 500 yards. It was not until improved 90mm ammunition was distributed in early 1945 that the M36 reached its potential.

The towed tank destroyer battalions employed the 3in. anti-tank gun M5 on carriage M6. This was an expedient design consisting of the 3in. gun as used on the M10 tank destroyer, mated to the carriage of the standard 105mm howitzer

The most common tank destroyer for much of the campaign in Europe was the M10 3in. GMC. Here, Co. A, 634th Tank Destroyer Battalion, fight their way into the outskirts of the German city of Aachen on October 14, 1944, while supporting the 1st Infantry Division. (NARA)

with a new protective shield. It was a mediocre design compared to its contemporaries such as the German PaK 40 75mm gun and the British 17-pdr. gun. It was heavier than both these other guns, half again as heavy as the German gun, yet it had inferior anti-tank penetration. The 3in. anti-tank gun was towed into action using the M3 halftrack, which also served to carry its ammunition and crew. The gun was too heavy and clumsy to be rapidly deployable, and this forced its use from prepared positions, defeating the basic tactical tenet of the tank destroyer doctrine. The T5E1 90mm anti-tank gun entered production in late 1944, but by the time it was ready for deployment to the ETO, towed guns had fallen out of favor. A single gun was sent to American forces deployed in Germany for trials in February 1945 but no combat units were reequipped with it during the war.

The M36 with a more powerful 90mm gun gradually replaced the M10 through the winter of 1944–45. The 740th Tank Battalion was rushed into combat with non-standard equipment in December 1944, including a few M36s, to support the 82nd Airborne Division in the Ardennes against the 1st SS-Panzer Division. They are seen here near Werbomont, Belgium, on December 20, 1944. (NARA)

Self-propelled tank destroyers in the ETO 1944–45											
	Jun 1944	Jul	Aug	Sep	Oct	Nov	Dec	Jan 45	Feb	Mar	Apr	May
M10	691	743	758	763	486	573	790	760	686	684	427	427
M18	146	141	176	170	189	252	306	312	448	540	427	427
M36					170	183	236	365	826	884	1,054	1,029
Total	837	884	934	933	845	1,008	1,332	1,437	1,960	2,108	1,908	1,883

Data as of 20th of each month

Command and control

The separate tank battalions

The initial plans to use the armored groups to control the separate tank battalions began to fall apart almost as soon as US troops landed in Normandy. Within days of the start of the Normandy campaign, infantry divisions were insisting that tank battalions be attached directly to them. This arrangement had been recommended for months before the start of the campaign by a number of senior US Army commanders, but McNair insisted on retaining the modular notion of support battalions. In the event, once the troops were committed to combat, the local theater commanders took control and they quickly acceded to the infantry division commanders. The armored groups became largely redundant. Some retained a role for specific missions, and they were often used to create specialized task forces. So, for example, in September 1944, the 3rd Armored Group with V Corps was assigned two tank battalions and given the mission of eliminating pillboxes along the Siegfried Line. When there were no specialized missions they were often used for non-combat missions, including the operation of rear area rest areas for armored units, supervision of specialized armor training such as flamethrower tanks or mine-exploders, and rear area military government functions. By the autumn of 1944, it had become evident that the armored divisions needed full-time headquarters for their third reserve combat

One of the first expedients to communicate between infantry and supporting tanks was to mount a tank SCR-509 radio on a packboard that could be carried by the infantry. The result was heavy and cumbersome, but was used until better alternatives became available. (NARA)

command (CCR), and divisional combat command headquarters happened to be patterned on the armored group HQ. So starting in late October 1944, the armored groups were gradually reassigned as CCR headquarters to the armored divisions starting with the assignment of the 3rd Armored Group as the CCR of the 5th Armored Division.

With the quick demise of the armored group concept, command of the separate tank battalions fell to the infantry division headquarters to which they were attached. In general, the pattern was for the tank battalion commander to become the armored advisor to the divisional commander. The usual deployment pattern was to assign each of the three medium tank companies to the three infantry regiments in each division. Some regiments used the entire tank company for missions, while others further distributed the tanks on the basis of one tank platoon per infantry battalion. The remainder of the tank battalion, usually called the "tank battalion (-)," was used in a variety of fashions. The light tank company presented a problem as most infantry units found that the 37mm gun and light armor of the M5A1 light tank made them less suitable for close infantry support than the M4 medium tanks. Some divisions assigned the light tank company to the divisional reconnaissance troop, while others kept them as a division mobile reserve where they could reinforce other tank companies. The M4 (105mm) assault guns in the HQ company were a popular asset to reinforce divisional artillery or as a form of reinforcing artillery that could be assigned as the need arose. Some battalions withdrew the assault guns from the three medium tank companies and consolidated them with the HQ company's assault guns to form a six-gun platoon.

In the summer of 1944, tank battalions began installing field telephones on the rear of their tanks to permit accompanying infantry to talk to the crew inside. This GI from the 81st Division is seen using the phone on a tank of the 709th Tank Battalion during fighting for Zweifall, Germany, on November 24, 1944.

The success or failure of the separate tank battalions was closely dependent on the skill of the divisional headquarters in the use of tanks. Many infantry divisions had not trained with a separate tank battalion and had a poor appreciation of proper tank tactics. Tank battalions were frequently misused as a result. Most often the problem was the overestimation of their capabilities and the lack of recognition of the vulnerability of the tanks, especially when used in small sub-units of company size or smaller. Divisional commanders would assign the battalion a mission without proper infantry or artillery support, leading to their speedy decimation. A postwar study of the problem noted that:

the combat team has become the keystone of all successful operations. The complexity of the new weapons and the limitations of each gives a complete interdependence of them on others to attain efficiency. Nothing is more helpless than a lone tank without artillery or infantry support. Its inherent blindness, its weight and size make it a natural target of all enemy fires. If friendly artillery is not coordinated, a hidden group of anti-tank guns will soon get it. Or if there is no infantry near, as soon as the tank slows down it becomes easy prey to an enemy infantryman with an anti-tank rocket. On the other hand, in operations where the tank–infantry–artillery and engineers are given their proper mission, one for which they have trained together as a team, the strength of each will complement the weakness of the other, thus making the strong concerted effort necessary for success.

Infantry divisions had the most success with tanks when the battalion was assigned for prolonged periods of time, which enabled joint training and an integration of the tank battalion headquarters within the divisional command. Some corps had the sense to semi-permanently attach tank battalions to a specific division and leave it attached for several months. In turn, this allowed the tank battalion to regularly assign specific companies to specific regiments on a long-term basis. Under these circumstances, lessons learned in combat led to more effective tactics, and a level of confidence was built up between the tankers and infantrymen. Throughout the European campaign, both the tank battalion commanders and the infantry division staff pleaded to make the tank battalions an organic part of each division. A General Board report after the war noted that if "the battalion had been an organic unit and trained with the division prior to combat, a better mutual understanding and spirit of cooperation would have always prevailed." However, since there were never enough tank battalions to permanently assign one to each infantry division, this did not occur until after the war.

One of the most serious technical impediments to tank–infantry cooperation was the lack of attention paid to tank–infantry communications at the small unit level. The problem of communications between the tank and infantry hinged on the incompatibility of tank and infantry radios. The US infantry in June 1944 was equipped with the hand-held SCR-586 "handie-talkie" at the platoon level. This was an AM radio transceiver, but the standard tank radios such as the SCR-508 were FM transceivers, so they could not talk to one another. The infantry employed the SCR-300 "walkie-talkie" FM radio at company level to communicate with battalion headquarters, but this operated in frequency bands different from the tank bands. US doctrine was that the tank company or battalion would communicate with higher infantry headquarters such as the infantry battalion, and then the communications would pass down through the chain of command via the company, and platoon. While this looked nice on paper, it was completely impractical in actual combat. Imagine for a moment that an infantryman spots an enemy anti-tank gun. Using the original scheme, his platoon would have to communicate this information to the company HQ, which would then have to transmit this to the infantry battalion, from there to the tank battalion, and then from the tank battalion down to the tank company. By the time this information had been received, the enemy anti-tank gun would have already done its damage.

A tank company supporting an infantry regiment was often broken up into tank platoons supporting specific infantry companies. The tank needed the immediate help of the infantry in identifying potential enemy threats such as the location of German anti-tank guns or anti-tank rocket teams, since the tank crew had poor visibility once the hatches were closed. Likewise, the infantry needed the immediate help of the tanks in suppressing German machine-gun fire when the infantry tried to advance. It was usually too dangerous and too noisy for a tank commander to remain exposed in the turret to receive shouted instructions from the infantry. Radio was the only practical solution since the infantry had no other means to communicate once the tank was buttoned up, but it was far too cumbersome to go through the proposed radio network to create effective tank–infantry communication at the small unit level.

This problem had been recognized prior to D-Day and steps were taken to adapt the infantry SCR-300 radio for use from the inside of a tank, a version later called the AN/VRC-3 radio. However, these were not available in the early summer of 1944. As a result, tank and infantry units began to experiment with a

By the autumn of 1944, tank phones had become commonplace and were generally mounted in a .30-cal. machine-gun ammo box as seen above the heads of these two GIs sheltering under the rear of an M4 medium near Gleich, Germany, on December 11, 1944. (NARA)

variety of local solutions. Some infantry units tried to give tank commanders spare SCR-586 radios to use from inside the tank, but this seldom worked as AM radios were vulnerable to interference inside a moving tank, which is why US tanks used FM radios. Other tank battalions took spare tank radios such as the SCR-509 and handed them over to infantry companies or battalion headquarters, which carried them into action on infantry packboards. This was not ideal as the radios were heavy and bulky, especially since they required a separate battery supply. Some units also experimented with placing infantry SCR-300 walkie-talkies inside tanks with the antenna sticking out through an open hatch. This was actually the most satisfactory of all the improvised radio solutions, but it could not be widely employed as the SCR-300 was only reaching service in the summer of 1944, and there was no surplus of these radios.

Another approach was to wire a field telephone into the tank. The army had already begun to plan a tank external telephone in May 1944, but development was not complete in time for the Normandy campaign. The first improvised attempts in France were very crude, with some tanks simply dragging a wire with a field telephone behind them for use by accompanying infantry. A more satisfactory approach was to wire the field telephone into the tank intercom system, but this was more complicated than it seemed since it could debilitate the tank interphone system without the proper switching. A design for wiring the tank with an EE-8 field telephone was finally developed by the First US Army in July 1944, and a conversion program was undertaken prior to the start of Operation Cobra at the end of July. The field telephone was mounted in an empty .30-cal. ammunition box welded to the back of the tank. An infantryman could walk behind the tank and communicate with the crew, pointing out targets. This solution was not ideal, since the infantryman could not accompany the tank once it began moving at normal speeds, and of course the infantryman was vulnerable to enemy fire. However, it proved to be better than nothing, and remained in widespread use through the European campaign.

The need for a tank–infantry radio was acknowledged by a June 15 TO&E change which authorized one AN/VRC-3 for each tank company HQ and two per tank platoon. These began arriving in September 1944, and were gradually introduced into the tank battalions by December. In combination with the tank-mounted field telephone, it helped to alleviate the problems with tank–infantry communication.

Besides the issue of infantry–tank cooperation, tank–artillery cooperation remained a problem for the separate tank battalions. Under the normal practice, each battalion was allotted a single artillery forward observer to coordinate supporting artillery strikes. This was far from ideal since the battalion usually had its three medium tank companies allotted to three different infantry regiments. In addition, the forward observers had not been trained in the use of tanks, and were frequently reluctant to ride in them to conduct their missions. As a result, the usual chain of command was for the tank platoon commanders to relay their fire requests to the supporting artillery via the infantry regiment. However, the tank officers did not have sufficient training to do this efficiently, and tank–artillery cooperation remained a problem through the European campaign. There were some experiments to alleviate this problem, for example an effort by the 743rd Tank Battalion in February–April 1945 to use a liaison aircraft to scout for the battalion and to call in artillery fire strikes.

The tank destroyer battalions

As in the case of tank battalions, there were tank destroyer groups intended to coordinate the actions of several tank destroyer battalions at army or corps level. These proved to be redundant for the same reasons as the tank and armored groups since the tank destroyer battalions were usually attached to infantry divisions rather than being kept in a corps reserve. The TD group staffs were often used on corps staffs to advise on anti-tank matters. The group itself was used for other missions often unrelated to their intended role, such as managing rear area defense troops, supervising corps rest areas, supervising corps traffic control, establishing motorized patrol in corps HQ areas, and supervising the formation of armored formations for protecting supply columns. On some rare occasions, the TD groups were assigned special combat missions, such as the use of the 2nd TD Group to coordinate tank destroyer battalions for the Roer River crossing in late February 1945.

Besides the groups, two tank destroyer brigade headquarters were organized, but the 2nd TD Brigade was disbanded in the US before being committed to action. The 1st TD Brigade served with Patton's Third Army in the Brittany campaign and was used to form Task Force A to seize the Breton ports. Like the tank destroyer groups, it was without a mission after this, and Patton used the staff in an advisory role in his headquarters.

With the tank destroyer groups largely irrelevant for most of the campaign, divisional control over the tank destroyer battalions was the norm. In the First Army, there was the widespread view that panzer attacks would be infrequent and so tank destroyers would often be assigned to supplement divisional artillery. As a result, it was frequently the practice to have the tank destroyers managed by the divisional artillery officer. This practice soon came into question when using self-propelled tank destroyers as these vehicles were used in much the same fashion as tanks, and so fell under control of the divisional G-3.

Tank destroyers had many of the same problems with communication as did the tanks. Their SCR-600 series radios could be tuned to the artillery radio nets, but as in the case of the tanks, not the infantry nets. Similar adaptations were made in the autumn to facilitate radio communication with the infantry, but the tank destroyer battalions had lower priority than the tank battalions.

The M20 armored utility car was widely used in tank destroyer battalions, both in a command role and by reconnaissance units. Here, the company commander of Co. A, 801st TD Battalion, leads his unit through Montebourg, France, on June 21, 1944. (MHI)

Tactics

The separate tank battalions

Tank battalion tactics were in a state of flux in June 1944 at the start of the campaign in Europe. However, once the fighting began in earnest in Normandy, the earlier ideas about using massed tank battalions under a tank group headquarters were quickly abandoned and the standard practice became to attach the battalions to the infantry divisions on a semi-permanent basis. The tactics of the tank battalions varied enormously from division to division, sometimes following established doctrine, but often extemporized to suit battlefield requirements. Rather than detail the theoretical tactics of the field manuals, this account will focus on actual tank tactics in some key combat missions.

Tank battalions in an amphibious assault

In preparation for Operation Neptune, the D-Day landings in Normandy, the ETOUSA (European Theater of Operations US Army) began to address the need for specialized armored units to assist in overcoming German coastal defenses. The British Army had been working on this problem since the ill-fated amphibious landing at Dieppe in 1942. As a result, the US Army tended to follow

An M4 dozer and M4A1 with wading trunks named Aide de Camp of Co. A, 741st Tank Battalion, on board an LCT on the way to Omaha Beach for the D-Day landings. (NARA)

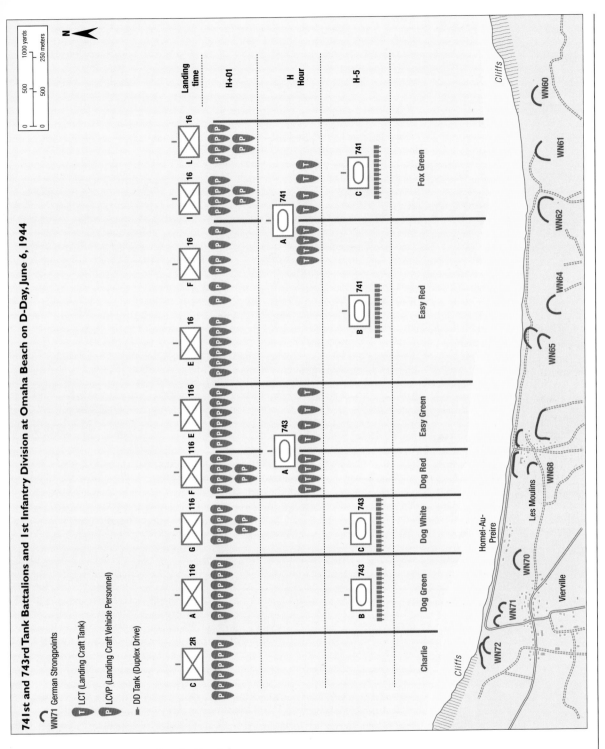

741st and 743rd Tank Battalions and 1st Infantry Division at Omaha Beach on D-Day, June 6, 1944

WN71 German Strongpoints

T LCT (Landing Craft Tank)

P LCVP (Landing Craft Vehicle Personnel)

DD Tank (Duplex Drive)

Tanks in amphibious assault—Omaha Beach

The plans for Operation Neptune included the support of both regimental combat teams at Omaha Beach by one tank battalion, with the 741st Tank Battalion supporting the 16th RCT on the eastern side and the 743rd supporting the 116th RCT on the western side. Each battalion deployed two companies with DD tanks and one company with M4 and M4A1 medium tanks with wading trunks. The DD tanks were supposed to be launched from 5,000 to 6,000 yards offshore, and to be the first US troops ashore five minutes before H-Hour, to be followed five minutes later by the remaining tank companies landing from LCTs. As it transpired, most of the DD tanks from the 741st Tank Battalion were swamped at sea, and the 743rd Tank Battalion's two DD companies landed directly on shore from their LCTs.

A pair of M4A1 DD amphibious tanks on the beach in southern France during Operation Dragoon on August 15, 1944. (NARA)

the British lead in regards to specialized equipment. However, due to McNair's strong aversion to specialized units, the US Army decided against following the British practice of a dedicated armored division for the specialized armor. Instead, the two armored groups of the First US Army, 3rd Armored Group with V Corps at Omaha Beach and the 6th Armored Group with the VII Corps at Utah Beach, were assigned to provide specialized training to their constituent tank battalions for operations on D-Day. Three tank battalions were assigned to the task, the 741st and 743rd Tank Battalions (Omaha Beach) and the 70th Tank Battalion (Utah Beach). At first, the US Army decided to use British equipment for this operation including Duplex Drive (DD) amphibious tanks, 25 Crab Flail mine-clearing tanks, and 100 Sherman Crocodile flamethrowing tanks. British industry was barely able to equip its own forces, and as a result the DD tanks had to be locally assembled in the US, and the mine-clearing and flamethrowing tanks were not available in time for the D-Day operations. The US Army rejected the use of the British Churchill AVRE combat engineer vehicle as it was developing its own equivalent, and also rejected the use of British bridging tanks, which it felt were unnecessary.

Training exercises with the DD "Donald Duck" tanks made it clear how vulnerable they were to rough water, and they were derisively called "30 tons of steel in a canvas bucket" by their crews. The commander of V Corps, Maj. Gen. Leonard Gerow, wanted them replaced with tanks fitted with deep wading trunks as had already been used with success at Sicily in 1943 and in subsequent amphibious operations in Italy. Since the training and equipping of the tank battalions was already well underway, a compromise was reached and each battalion was deployed with two companies of DD tanks, and one company with deep wading equipment. Gerow's skepticism proved well founded, and the DD tanks were largely a failure on D-Day due to rough weather in the English

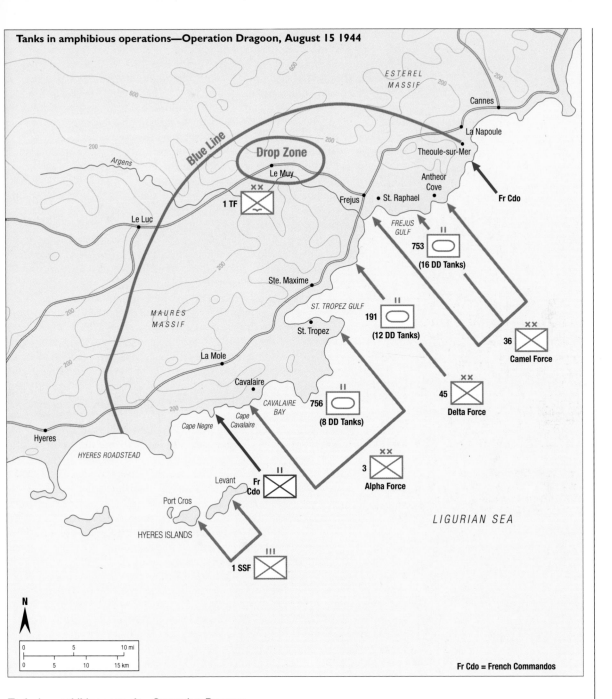

Tanks in amphibious assault—Operation Dragoon

Although less well known than the amphibious assault in Normandy, tank battalions also supported the landings on the French Riviera on August 15, 1944, when the US Seventh Army invaded southern France. Each of the assaulting divisions was assigned a tank battalion, with each of these battalions having about a company of DD tanks. The eight DD tanks of the 756th Tank Battalion with Alpha Force disembarked about 2,500 yards from the beach and swam to shore, with one being sunk by wash from a passing landing craft and another by an underwater mine. Two tanks from this unit were involved in fighting against German pillboxes, Of the 12 DD tanks with the 191st Tank Battalion in the center with Delta Force, four swam ashore from 75 yards at H-hour (0800hrs), while the remaining eight were landed from their LCTs directly on shore. Of the 16 DD tanks of the 753rd Tank Battalion with Camel Force, eight swam ashore in the initial wave and the remaining eight arrived in the early afternoon, and were landed directly on shore. There was a skirmish between these tanks and a German self-propelled gun, which was knocked out. There was significantly less resistance on these beaches than at Normandy, but mines disabled at least five tanks.

Channel. The US Army's Armored Vehicle Engineer (AVE) was not ready in time for D-Day, and in its place two specialized tanks were selected. To breach the sea walls, some M4 tanks were equipped with the new T40 7.2in. demolition rocket launcher. These were first issued to the 70th Tank Battalion in May 1944, but they were clumsy to use and no more effective than normal tank gun fire. As a result, none were deployed on D-Day. A far more successful innovation was the dozer tank, a normal M4 tank fitted with a special bulldozer blade for clearing tank obstructions and filling in anti-tank ditches. These were deployed on a scale of four per battalion and proved to be the most successful bit of US specialized tank equipment used on D-Day.

During the landings, the 741st Tank Battalion supported the 16th Regimental Combat Team (RCT) on the eastern side of Omaha Beach, and the 743rd supported the 116th RCT on the western side. The officers in charge of the two companies of DD tanks decided to launch the amphibians from 6,000 yards off shore in spite of the heavy sea state, and all sank except for two that swam to shore and three that were landed directly on the beach from their Landing Craft Tank (LCT). In contrast, the navy lieutenant commanding the LCT flotilla carrying the 743rd recommended landing on the beach, and so nearly all their tanks arrived safely. The weather conditions off Utah Beach were not as rough, and the 70th Tank Battalion disembarked their DD tanks from only 1,000 yards due to a timing problem, and most made it to shore. Of the 96 DD tanks deployed on D-Day, 60 reached the shore, while nearly all the 48 M4 tanks with deep-wading trucks reached the shore. The planned tactic for D-Day was for the tanks to remain in the water up to the height of their turrets with the sea providing protection for their hulls. While some tanks did use this tactic, most ended up driving to shore and carrying on the fight from dry land. The tanks proved very useful in engaging the German defenses, and one of the infantry commanders noted that the 743rd Tank Battalion had "saved the day. They shot the hell out of the Germans and got the hell shot out of them." The badly decimated 741st lost most of its tanks battling German pillboxes and would not have had any by day's end but for the arrival of four reserve tanks in the afternoon. The 70th Tank Battalion was instrumental in clearing out German opposition on Utah Beach and spearheading the assault off the beach, being awarded the Presidential Unit Citation for their performance on D-Day.

DD tanks were later shipped to the Mediterranean theater for use during the August 1944 Operation Dragoon landings in southern France. A total of 36 DD tanks were used during the August 15 landings with three tank battalions, the 191st, 753rd, and 756th Tank Battalions. Of these, 20 swam ashore and the remaining 16 were landed directly on the beach by their LCTs. The use of DD tanks was much more successful in Dragoon than in Neptune because the sea conditions were much calmer and the German opposition was negligible.

The army subsequently concluded that DD tanks were not suitable for use in heavy sea conditions but some were retained in theater for later river-crossing operations. The three tank battalions were subsequently reequipped with conventional M4 and M4A1 medium tanks for the fighting in Normandy.

The battle of the hedgerows

The US Army had failed to anticipate how difficult the hedgerow terrain in Normandy would be for the conduct of offensive operations. A thick, dense hedge, locally called bocage, which protected the field from the coastal winds, surrounded each farm field. These served as natural defensive fortifications and were skilfully exploited by the German defenders. The difficulties in forcing the German infantry out of the bocage led the infantry divisions to insist on the attachment of tanks to assist the infantry.

The tanks proved very useful in helping the infantry assault the dug-in German defenders, but they were not totally effective in breaking through the German lines. The bocage posed a major mobility problem since the tanks trying to drive over the hedge exposed their thin underbelly to German anti-tank fire, and German anti-tank guns easily blocked the small number of narrow country roads.

The bocage fighting highlighted the lack of attention that had been paid to realistic tank–infantry training and led to local attempts to improve the situation. Many units found that even a day of joint training before a major operation provided a major improvement since officers from both units were able to better understand the capabilities, requirements, and limitations of tanks supporting infantry. In some divisions, it became the practice to link specific tank companies with specific infantry regiments. At the small unit level, most units found that tank–infantry coordination was best managed by assigning a rifle squad to each tank platoon for direct support. The squad was responsible for protecting the tanks from close-in attack by German infantry, and regular attachment of the squad avoided the need to continually retrain new units in tank–infantry cooperation.

Plans to conduct a major breakout operation in late July, codenamed Operation Cobra, accelerated the effort to develop tactics to deal with the bocage. A number of experiments were conducted using improvised hedge cutters made from steel beams to permit tanks to plow through the hedges. One of the first of these, dubbed the "Salad Fork," was tested during an offensive near St. Lô on July 11, 1944. The 29th Division commander, Maj. Gen. Charles Gebhardt, created a special training area to help develop tank–infantry tactics with the attached 747th Tank Battalion. The tactics were dubbed "one squad, one tank, one field" with the idea being that a single tank with a hedge-buster would penetrate a hedgerow, followed up closely by an infantry squad under the covering fire of the tank.

A T1E1 Rhinoceros hedgerow cutter fitted to the front of an M10 3in. GMC in preparation for the Operation Cobra breakout. (MHI)

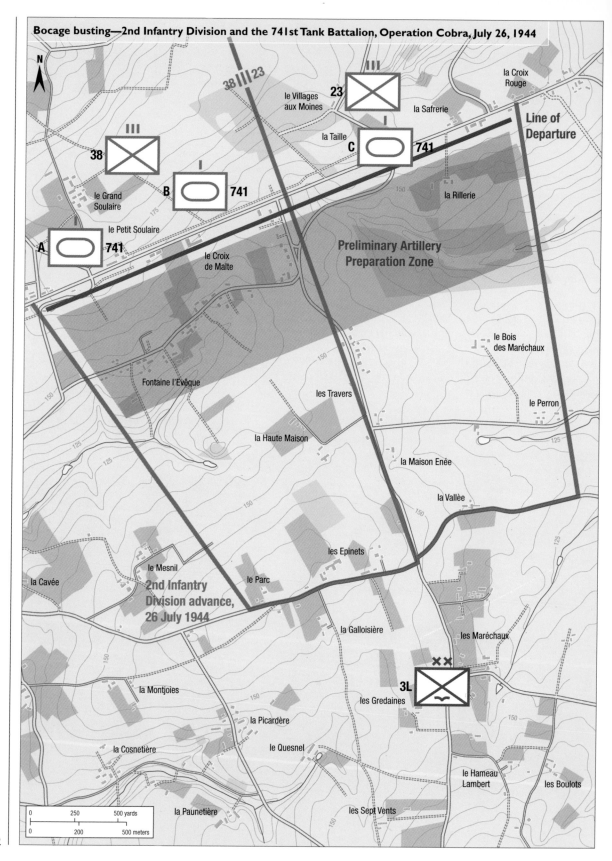

Bocage busting—2nd Infantry Division and the 741st Tank Battalion, Operation Cobra, July 26, 1944

N

38 ||| 23

le Villages
aux Moines

23

la Croix
Rouge

la Safrerie

Line of
Departure

la Taille

C

741

38

le Grand
Soulaire

B

741

la Rillerie

le Petit Soulaire

A

741

le Croix
de Malte

Preliminary Artillery
Preparation Zone

le Bois
des Maréchaux

Fontaine l'Evêque

le Perron

les Travers

la Haute Maison

la Maison Enée

la Vallèe

les Epinets

la Cavée

le Mesnil

2nd Infantry
Division advance,
26 July 1944

le Parc

la Galloisière

les Maréchaux

la Montjoies

3L

les Gredaines

la Picardère

la Cosnetière

le Quesnel

le Hameau
Lambert

les Boulots

la Paunetière

les Sept Vents

| 0 | 250 | 500 yards |
| 0 | 200 | 500 meters |

Sgt. Curtis Culin subsequently developed a better hedge-buster, and local production of the "rhino" was undertaken by First US Army ordnance units to equip several hundred tanks prior to Operation Cobra. The breakthrough tactics varied from unit to unit. For example, the 741st Tank Battalion supporting the 2nd Infantry Division developed a tactic called a tank sortie. The infantry remained under cover along the line-of-departure and an assault zone about 500 yards deep was beaten down by divisional artillery firing airburst rounds. The tanks crunched through the bocage using the rhinos, and the artillery kept the German defenders in their trenches while the tanks attacked them. After the tanks penetrated 500 yards in about 20 minutes, some returned to the line-of-departure to escort the infantry to rout out any remaining defenders. The process then continued and the German defenses were systematically overcome.

The new tactics were instrumental in the first few days of fighting when Operation Cobra began on July 26. Although the infantry penetrations of the German defenses were not as deep as had been hoped, they so disrupted the German defenses that the corps commander decided to commit his two reserve armored divisions to begin the breakout and exploitation phase. Cobra was a resounding success and the US Army finally fought its way out of the constricted terrain of Normandy towards the open terrain on the approaches to Paris. A total of 12 separate tank battalions were used during Operation Cobra, and they suffered relatively modest losses of only 49 tanks in a week of fighting due to the improved tactics.

The mobile campaign that followed in August was a complete contrast to the two months of hard fighting in the enclosed terrain of Normandy. Tank tactics were improvised, and many units formed small task forces consisting of a platoon or more of tanks supporting their infantry battalions, with the infantry forming assault groups that would ride the tanks to speed up the assault.

Although the various Rhino devices are most famous for their role in Operation Cobra, tank dozers like the one seen here were also extensively used for bocage busting in July 1944. (NARA)

Attacking a fortified zone

By mid-September, Bradley's US 12th Army Group had advanced past Paris, through Belgium, and into the Belgian–German border area around Aachen. The Siegfried Line campaign in the autumn of 1944 provided a new series of challenges for the separate tank battalions. The Wehrmacht had fortified the border area in the late 1930s, though the defenses were far from uniform. Some of the Westwall was erected in heavily forested areas, while other sections ran near towns and industrial areas.

Specialized equipment to assist in attacking fortified lines was generally lacking, as the US Army did not expect it would reach the Siegfried Line so soon. There were plans underway to mount the E4-5 flamethrower on a scale of one per tank platoon, but trials in Normandy in July were unimpressive and tank officers described the system as "pathetic." Four E4-5 flamethrowers were fitted to tanks of the 70th Tank Battalion on September 11, 1944, and used to attack a German pillbox three days later. This configuration was found seriously inadequate as the tank had to approach to within 25 yards of the pillbox, and, even after using up its fuel, the pillbox was not knocked out. Plans to deploy the British Crocodile system mounted on the Sherman tank had floundered and only four were delivered. These were first used in February 1945 during Operation Grenade against the citadel in Jülich.

None of the tank battalions had received any detailed training on how to assault fortifications, and so tactics had to be improvised. The 3rd Armored

Crews of the 735th Tank Battalion attach a demolition Snake to their tank prior to the assault on Ft. Driant. This consisted of up to 400ft of explosive-packed tubing that was pushed in front of the tank and detonated to blow gaps in minefields. The Snakes did not prove useful in the attack due to the difficulty of pushing them to the objective. (NARA)

Group was assigned to develop suitable tactics, and it included the 741st and 747th Tank Battalions. A fairly typical example of its work took place in mid-September when the 28th Division was assigned to widen a gap in the Siegfried Line between the towns of Groskampenberg and Heckuscheid. Task Force M formed special assault companies consisting of a medium tank company reinforced with 105mm assault guns and one or more dozer tanks. These were used in conjunction with a company of infantry and some divisional engineers. The tanks would assault one pillbox at a time and once the fire from the bunker had been suppressed by tank fire, the infantry would advance to hold the pillbox. If the German defenders did not surrender, engineer demolition teams would then destroy the pillbox, or a tank dozer would bury the embrasures and access doors to prevent their further use. The task force overran about 50 pillboxes during four days of fighting on September 19–22. Other tank battalions and their parent infantry divisions in neighboring sectors devised similar tank–infantry–engineer tactics.

Besides the fighting for the Siegfried Line by the First and Ninth Armies along the Dutch–Belgian–German frontier, Patton's Third Army also had its share of fighting for fortified areas during its autumn campaign in Lorraine, including the struggle for the fortified city of Metz. After failing to seize the city in early September, Third Army was faced with the unenviable task of reducing one of the oldest and strongest border fortifications along the French–German frontier. There were a total of 28 major forts and fortified areas around the city, consisting of both the original French defenses, and newer positions built by the Germans after 1870 and again after 1940. Among the most critical elements of this defensive network was Ft. Driant, positioned on a hill southwest of Metz that commanded the main river crossing over the Moselle. After fire from the fort prevented the 5th Infantry Division from securing a bridgehead over the Moselle, plans began to assault the fort using a combined infantry–tank attack. An initial probing attack was conducted on September 27, 1944, using the 2/11th Infantry without tank support. The infantry were unable to reach the main fortifications due to the interlocking fields of fire from previously undiscovered pillboxes as well as heavy artillery fire. The next attack was launched on October 3 with the support of the 735th Tank Battalion. Besides a variety of infantry demolition devices such as pole charges, the attack was the first to use "Snakes," an explosive-filled pipe pushed in front of a tank to blow gaps in the barbed wire obstructions around the fort. The attack was also supported by three M12 155mm GMC self-propelled guns of the 558th Field Artillery Battalion, which were placed in special sandbagged parapets to provide heavy caliber, direct fire support against the embrasures of the fort. Three companies of the 11th Infantry were assigned to the attack, each supported by a tank platoon equipped with M4 (76mm) tanks with special concrete-penetrating ammunition, as well as M4 (105mm) assault guns and dozer tanks.

The attack began before dawn, but the Snakes proved to be very difficult to move into position and were ineffective. Artillery bombardment of the fort proved futile due to its excellent design, and the tank–infantry teams were decimated by artillery fire from neighboring forts and by German tank-killer teams armed with anti-tank rockets. The attack force was pinned down in intense fighting within the defensive zone of Ft. Driant, forcing the 5th Infantry Division to commit reinforcements on October 5. Although the tanks attempted to support the attack, they were decimated in close combat with the bunkers. The fighting degenerated into savage infantry actions, and, after a week of attacks, only two barracks had been captured while the five main casements remained in German hands. The attack was broken off on October 10, and the fort did not fall until December 8, after the surrender of Metz itself. The ill-fated assault on Ft. Driant highlighted the lack of US Army preparations for the attack of fortified areas in terms of specialized equipment. The US Army lacked a specialized infantry tank better able to survive under intense gunfire, and had

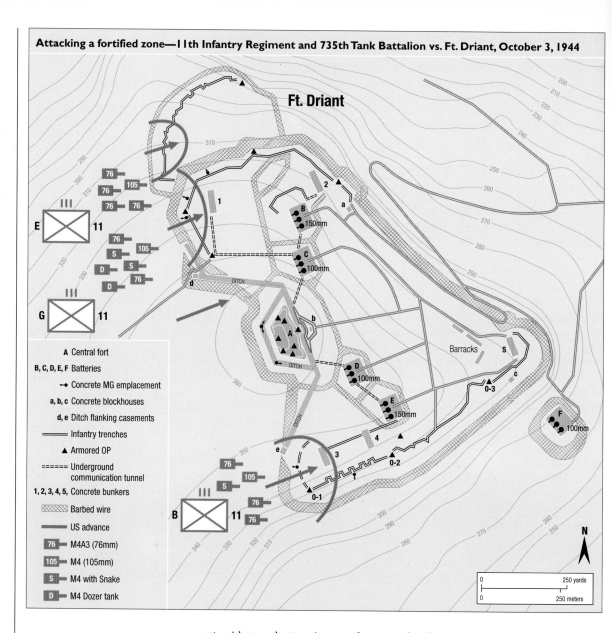

Attacking a fortified zone—11th Infantry Regiment and 735th Tank Battalion vs. Ft. Driant, October 3, 1944

Ft. Driant

E 11

G 11

A Central fort
B, C, D, E, F Batteries
➤ Concrete MG emplacement
a, b, c Concrete blockhouses
d, e Ditch flanking casements
═══ Infantry trenches
▲ Armored OP
====== Underground communication tunnel
1, 2, 3, 4, 5, Concrete bunkers
▨▨▨ Barbed wire
━━━ US advance
76 M4A3 (76mm)
105 M4 (105mm)
S M4 with Snake
D M4 Dozer tank

B 11

Barracks 5

N

0   250 yards
0   250 meters

not paid enough attention to other specialized equipment such as tank-mounted flamethrowers. However, the classic fortifications of the Metz type were a rarity in the European campaign, and the less substantial pillboxes and bunkers of the Siegfried Line proved more vulnerable to determined tank–infantry–engineer attacks.

No matter how formidable the defenses of the Siegfried Line might have been, natural obstructions still could be a far more troublesome defensive barrier for tank operations. No tract of land caused the US Army more problems in the autumn of 1944 than the Hürtgen Forest. The fighting for the Hürtgenwald was started by the 9th Infantry Division and the supporting 746th Tank Battalion in late October as part of the First Army's attempt to reach the Roer River. The forest fighting proved unusually costly and tanks provided little solace for the infantry. The forest was crisscrossed with many narrow roads and forest paths, but they were frequently too narrow for tanks, and could be readily mined or defended by German anti-tank teams. After the 9th Infantry Division was decimated, other infantry divisions were fed into the "forested hell," including the 28th Infantry

Division with its 707th Tank Battalion. Between November 2 and 8, the 707th had all but eight of its tanks put out of action in the furious fighting for Schmidt. In the end, the two months of fighting in the Hürtgenwald was a bloody slugging match between infantry and artillery, with tanks playing only a marginal role. Two of the tank battalions smashed up in the Hürtgenwald, the 70th and 707th, were sent back to the Ardennes to recuperate, only to be caught up in the maelstrom of the Ardennes offensive in mid-December.

By the autumn of 1944, the 12th Army Group was seriously short of tank battalions as the number of infantry divisions outstripped the number of tank battalions. As a result, on November 4, 1944, Eisenhower's headquarters ordered that the six battalions configured for night fighting with Leaflet tanks be reorganized. Four became normal tank battalions, and the other two were reorganized into a new Special Mine Exploder (SMX) configuration. The US Army had received a small number of British Crab flail tanks to deal with the mine threat in the summer of 1944, and some had been deployed with little success by the 747th Tank Battalion in July 1944 near St. Lô. The new SMX organization was intended to concentrate these specialized vehicles so that the crews had proper training in their operation. The original organization of these battalions was a company of 18 M32 TRVs pushing the T1E1 "Earthworm" mine exploder, and two companies with 12 M4 medium tanks pushing the T1E3 "Aunt Jemima" mine exploder plus six M4 dozer tanks. The 738th Tank Battalion (SMX) was deployed with the First US Army and the 739th with the Ninth US Army. The Seventh US Army already had the 6638th Mine Field Clearance Company, a specialized unit formed earlier in Italy. There was very

The US Seventh Army deployed its specialized mine-clearing tanks with the 6638th Mine Field Clearance Company, a unit previously formed in Italy in 1944 for this mission. Here a T1E3 "Aunt Jemima" mine exploder is seen near Nancy, France, in the late summer of 1944. (NARA)

A M32B1 with T1E1 mine rollers from Company B, 738th Tank Battalion (SMX), near Faymonville, Belgium, on January 16, 1945, during the concluding phase of the Battle of the Bulge. (MHI)

little use of these units until January 1945 due to the wet ground conditions along the German frontier that made it very difficult to use mine rollers effectively. The two SMX battalions were reorganized again in February 1945 to use other specialized armor including DD tanks for the upcoming Rhine crossing, and their old Leaflet tanks for defense of the Rhine crossings against German night attack.

Besides the American-designed mine exploders, US tank units in the ETO obtained a small number of British Crab flail tanks. This example with the 739th Tank Battalion (SMX) is seen in operation near Vicht on the Roer River approaches on February 21, 1945, during Operation Grenade.

The E4-5 flamethrower was mounted in some M4 medium tanks in the autumn of 1944 in place of the hull machine gun. This M4 tank of the 747th Tank Battalion is seen moments after having set a barn afire near Schleiden, Germany, on January 5, 1945. (NARA)

The rare M4 Crocodile flamethrower tanks were used by the 739th Tank Battalion (SMX) to support the 29th Division's attack on the citadel in Jülich on February 24. These towed an armored trailer that contained the fuel. (NARA)

Tank battalions in the defense

Separate tank battalions were often used to help bolster infantry division defenses throughout the 1944–45 campaign. However, the only large-scale defensive use of the tank battalions in this role was in response to the German Ardennes offensive in December 1944. Since Normandy, the 741st Tank Battalion, the same unit that had lost so many DD tanks at Omaha Beach, had supported the 2nd Infantry Division. By this stage of the war, the tank battalion had become well integrated into the operational procedures of the division, which enabled both units to cooperate effectively in the difficult circumstances of the Battle of the Bulge.

59

A white-washed M18 76mm GMC supporting the 2nd Infantry Division during operations in Krinkelt, Belgium, in late January 1945 during the Ardennes counter-offensive. The village had earlier been the scene of an intense house-to-house fight that had deflected the initial 12th SS-Panzer Division attack. (NARA)

The 2nd Infantry Division was not in the path of the German offensive, but somewhat to the north of the German attack sector. When the inexperienced 99th Division came under intense German attack by the 1st SS-Panzer Corps on December 16, 1944, the 2nd Infantry Division was alerted to send reinforcements southward to help. The 38th Infantry Regiment was dispatched to the twin villages of Krinkelt–Rocherath, accompanied by about 20 tanks of the 741st Tank Battalion. The tanks deployed in scattered positions, with the heaviest concentration in the open fields between the two villages. On the morning of December 17, they began to encounter lead elements of the 12th SS-Panzer Division, knocking out a halftrack and armored car along the Krinkelt road, and three PzKpfw IVs near Wirtzfeld. One of the battalion's tanks was lost after dark in a firefight with German armor in Krinkelt. Panthers began to appear on the outskirts of Rocherath, and in a close-range tank duel two M4 tanks were knocked out, but put two of the three attacking panzers out of action as well. About four Panthers penetrated into Rocherath after dark, knocking out three M4 tanks but losing one Panther to an infantry bazooka team. The German panzer attack against Rocherath began in earnest on the morning of December 18, with Panther tanks clanking into the village about 150 yards from the battalion headquarters on the northeast side of Rocherath. Two immobile M4 tanks with maintenance problems were positioned in alleys near the HQ and ambushed the advancing German column, claiming five Panthers, and the sixth was knocked out by a mobile M4. The tank fighting in the villages took place at very close range, with some tanks supported by bazooka-armed infantry. By December 19, the US defenses around Krinkelt–Rocherath were crumbling, but the 38th Infantry Regiment had delayed the 12th SS-Panzer Division and a volksgrenadier division long enough

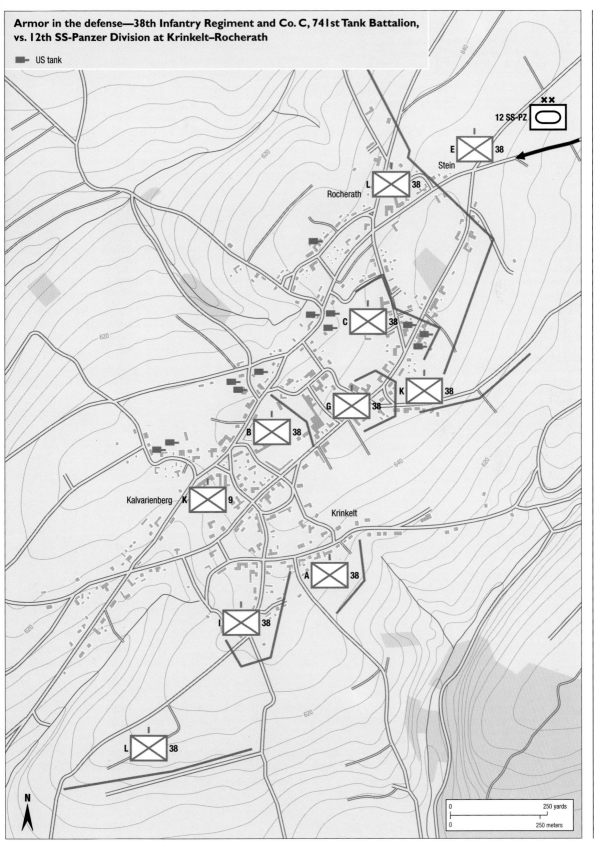

Armor in the defense—38th Infantry Regiment and Co. C, 741st Tank Battalion, vs. 12th SS-Panzer Division at Krinkelt–Rocherath

US tank

12 SS-PZ

E 38

Stein

L 38

Rocherath

C 38

K 38

G 38

B 38

Kalvarienberg K 9

Krinkelt

A 38

I 38

L 38

N

0   250 yards
0   250 meters

for critical reinforcements to arrive at Butgenbach. In the late afternoon of December 19, the US forces in the twin villages began withdrawing with eight tanks from Company B, 741st Tank Battalion forming a rearguard on the road towards Wirtzfeld. During the fighting, the badly outnumbered 741st Tank Battalion claimed to have destroyed 27 panzers (mostly Panthers), one Jagdpanzer IV, two armored cars, two halftracks, and two trucks for a loss of eight tanks and eight tankers killed. The battalion was later awarded the Presidential Unit Citation for their actions at Rocherath. The 12th SS-Panzer Division next encountered a regiment from the 1st Infantry Division at Dom Butgenbach, supported by a company of the 745th Tank Battalion. In the ensuing fight, the advance of the 12th SS-Panzer Division was finally halted in this sector, with Company C, 745th Tank Battalion claiming 13 tanks and one jagdpanzer.

The 707th Tank Battalion, rebuilt after the Hürtgenwald fighting, was supporting the 28th Division when the full weight of the German Fifth Panzer Army struck it. During the fighting on December 17, Company D was wiped out trying to reinforce Marnach, and 16 M4 tanks were lost after knocking out six panzers and four jagdpanzers. The following day, Company C covered the withdrawal of the 109th Infantry while the remnants of the rest of the battalion were amalgamated into a composite company to support the 110th Infantry and divisional HQ at Wiltz. By December 20, the battalion had been reduced to a handful of tanks with most of its personnel killed, wounded, or missing. Yet the defense of the approaches to Bastogne by the 28th Division and the supporting 707th Tank Battalion played a key role in delaying the German offensive, and bought the First US Army precious time to move armored reinforcements into Bastogne. Another Hürtgenwald veteran, the 70th

The 707th Tank Battalion, already decimated from the Hürtgen Forest fighting, was nearly wiped out while waging a last-ditch defense in the Ardennes with the 28th Division in December 1944. One of its tanks is seen in the debris of Clerf and to the right is a knocked-out German StuG III assault gun. (NARA)

Tank Battalion, was near the southern shoulder of the German assault, and the harried 4th Infantry Division later praised its role in the fighting as "the most outstanding tank support that this infantry regiment has ever witnessed."

Another D-Day veteran, the 743rd Tank Battalion, was supporting the 30th Division, which was sent into the Ardennes to stop Kampfgruppe Peiper of the 1st SS-Panzer Division. The 743rd deployed in the hill country along the Ambleve Valley, finally establishing a defensive line west of Stoumont. Its neighbor, the 740th Tank Battalion, was the least experienced US tank battalion in the theater. It had been one of the special night-fighting tank battalions with Leaflet tanks converted to a normal tank battalion. But when it arrived in Belgium in December, it had no tanks of its own and was told to go to an ordnance depot and take whatever it could find. It located 14 British Sherman tanks, five M4A1 DD tanks, an M36 90mm tank destroyer and two brand-new M24 light tanks. The battalion entered combat alongside the 30th Division during the fighting against Kampfgruppe Peiper near La Gleize, helping to prevent the breakout of the other spearhead unit of the 1st SS-Panzer Corps. The performance of the separate tank battalions in the Ardennes has seldom received much attention since most accounts focus on the infantry divisions they were supporting and most of the battalions were deployed piecemeal, a company at a time. Nevertheless, the presence of experienced tank battalions helped stiffen the US defense.

River-crossing operations

Few military operations are as difficult as contested river-crossing operations. Following the Ardennes campaign, the US Army resumed its offensive operations against Germany and confronted a series of major river obstacles including the Roer and the Rhine. The Roer River had been the objective of the US Army since the autumn, and the seizure of the Roer dams had been the rationale for the bloody Hürtgen fighting. The Roer River was a key objective since it lay about 25 miles west of the Rhine and had to be breached before the Rhine itself could be assaulted. The US Ninth Army planned to leap over the Roer in late

The first Ninth Army tank over the Roer was this M4A3 (76mm) tank from the 771st Tank Battalion moving over the treadway bridge at Linnich on February 24. During Operation Grenade, the battalion provided fire support for the 84th Division from the hilly area in the background. (NARA)

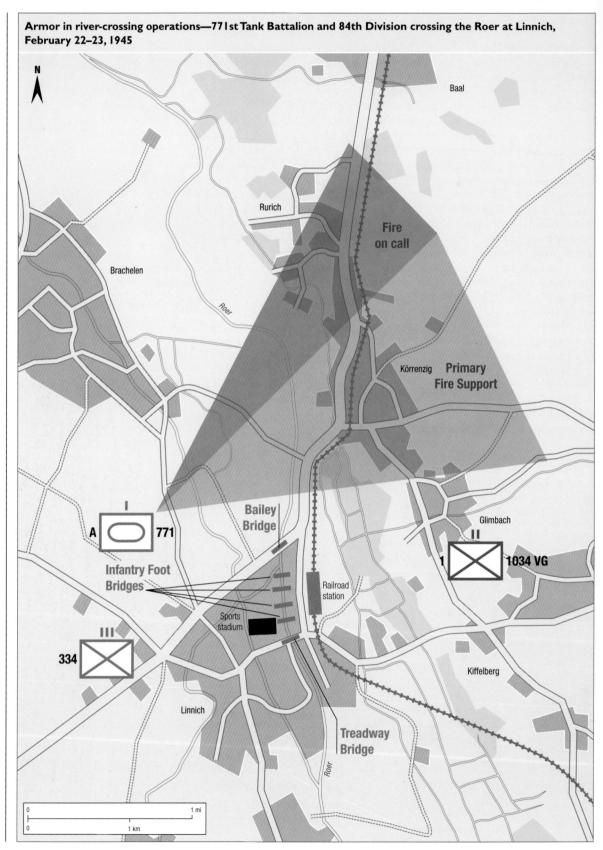

Armor in river-crossing operations—771st Tank Battalion and 84th Division crossing the Roer at Linnich, February 22–23, 1945

N

Baal

Rurich

Fire
on call

Brachelen

Roer

Körrenzig

Primary
Fire Support

Bailey
Bridge

A ⎯ 771

Glimbach

1 ‖ 1034 VG

Infantry Foot
Bridges

Railroad
station

Sports
stadium

334 ⫴

Kiffelberg

Linnich

Treadway
Bridge

Roer

0   1 mi
0   1 km

February in a carefully planned assault called Operation Grenade. As a part of this operation, the 84th Division was assigned to the crossing at Linnich, supported by the 771st Tank Battalion.

The Linnich crossing was typical of US river-crossing tactics. The initial operation was a combined infantry–engineer operation aimed at putting troops across the river by boat, followed by footbridges, and finally by treadway bridges heavy enough to support vehicular traffic. The operation began on the night of February 20–21, with artillery preparations that were feints to discover German reactions. A second night of artillery preparations followed so that by the third night, February 22–23, the German defenders of 1./Volksgrenadier Regt. 1034, 59th Volksgrenadier Division, were convinced it was simply another feint and not a real attack. That night, every available gun in the division took part in the preparation, including antiaircraft guns, and the weapons of both the supporting tank and tank destroyer battalions. The assault companies of the 334th Infantry set off in their boats at 0340hrs, and by 0610hrs, the 1/334th Infantry had advanced 2,000 yards beyond the bridgehead and seized the town of Korrenzig. During this phase of the operation, the artillery barrage lifted, and the 771st Tank Battalion continued to provide direct fire support since it was positioned on a slight rise outside the town where it overlooked the river-crossing sites. By 1450hrs, all three infantry battalions of the 334th Infantry were across and a bridgehead 4,000 yards wide and 1,000 yards deep had been established, permitting the engineers to begin assembling a treadway bridge. Although this was completed, it was knocked out shortly after it was completed by a Luftwaffe attack. As a result, the planned armored support for the

An M4A3 (76mm) from the 771st Tank Battalion leads a column through Linnich on February 24, 1945, the day after the 84th Division seized the town at the start of Operation Grenade. The first vehicular bridge was put across the Roer River hours before, and tanks and tank destroyers were rushed into the town in anticipation of a German counterattack as both 9th and 11th Panzer Divisions were stationed to the west of Cologne.

Many of the M4A1 DD tanks available in the spring of 1945 were not in very good condition, so as often as not they went over the Rhine by ferry or pontoon bridge as is the case of this M4A1 DD of the 748th Tank Battalion at Boppard, Germany, March 26, 1944. (NARA)

bridgehead was not possible until the bridge was reconstructed on February 24. The 334th Infantry faced a German counterattack supported by assault guns without tank support shortly before midnight.

The bridge was completed for a third time around 1120hrs on February 24 and was almost immediately attacked by Me 262 jet fighters, but both were shot down by US artillery. The tanks finally began crossing shortly before noon, and the entire battalion was over the Roer by the end of the day. The availability of tanks allowed the 335th Infantry to assault Doveren and Doverhahn, but the infantry did not follow the tanks into the towns, and the tankers had to dismount and clear German panzerfaust anti-tank teams from the buildings on their own. A company from the 771st Tank Battalion also assisted in repulsing an attack by a battalion of infantry from the 183rd Volksgrenadier Division after midnight. The following day, the 2/335th Infantry moved out of Doveren supported by Company C of the 771st Tank Battalion, and overran a series of prepared German defenses. After passing through woods on the approaches to the village of Houverath, a column of six PzKpfw IV tanks attacked the infantry, but C/771st Tank Battalion beat them off. The town was badly smashed up by tank fire and occupied by the infantry within 40 minutes of the start of the attack. One of the infantry officers later wrote that "it was a perfect operation, the sort of thing they dream of at Fort Benning [the US infantry school]."

The smooth conduct of Operation Grenade by the 84th Division was largely due to an experienced infantry–tank team, which had been fighting alongside one another since the fighting in the Ardennes in December 1944. However, it also highlighted the problem presented by the interlude between the time the infantry first established the bridgehead and the time that tank

support arrived. In this case, it took 36 hours, and the 84th Division was lucky that the Germans were unable to counterattack the bridgehead with enough force. The US Army appreciated this problem, and plans were already underway to speed the reinforcement of the infantry in forthcoming river-crossing operations.

In anticipation of the Rhine operations, in October 1944 a special river training and testing center was established on the Loire River near Orléans, which included a DD tank-training program. The US 12th Army Group began steps to collect sufficient DD amphibious tanks in November 1944. Only about 115 M4A1 DD tanks were still available, so these were supplemented with British Sherman III (M4A2) and Sherman V (M4A4) DD tanks. In the event, far fewer DD tanks were used for the Rhine crossing than originally anticipated. Co. C, 736th Tank Battalion with the Ninth Army crossed the Rhine on March 23–24, 1945, while supporting the 83rd Division. This company swam across the river shortly before dawn and so was already in place prior to the infantry crossing. The bridgehead was further reinforced with tanks by moving two companies from the 743rd Tank Battalion over the river using ferries. The 748th Tank Battalion was nearly fully equipped with 51 DD tanks, but a long road march to the Rhine damaged the specialized equipment and only 18 were floatable. A total of eight were launched across the Rhine with the 89th Division near Oppenheim on March 23–24, 1945, with one sinking. Ten more were ferried across. Although other tank battalions received DD tanks for possible river-crossing operations, the Rhine crossing was the last time that the DD tanks were used in an amphibious role during the war.

Another method to deploy tanks rapidly into a bridgehead, short of the use of amphibious tanks, was to employ tank rafts. These were created using engineer pontoons and sections of treadway bridging, and a "sea mule," a small engineer boat used in bridging operations, powered the raft. The 743rd Tank Battalion used this approach when crossing the Rhine on March 24, 1945. However, this tactic required significant pre-planning in order to have the equipment ready, and required an area of riverbank relatively free of enemy opposition where the rafts could be assembled. Other battalions used landing craft that had been moved to the Rhine on tank transporters prior to the operation.

The 747th Tank Battalion was reequipped with amphibious tractors (amtracs) prior to the Rhine crossing while supporting the 30th Division. Each of its four companies received 17 LVT-2 and eight LVT-4 amtracs on March 6, 1945. Starting on March 24, 1945, they were used to transport two battalions of the 30th Division and one battalion of the 79th Division over the Rhine, as well as supplies and reinforcements. They faced little opposition, although two amtracs were damaged by artillery fire. This was one of the only large-scale combat uses of the amtrac in the ETO.

Tanks as artillery

The T34 Calliope multiple rocket launcher was one idea to enhance the value of tanks in the indirect fire support mission. However, most tank officers thought that the cumbersome launcher distracted the tanks from their primary missions. (NARA)

Separate tank battalions were sometimes used to provide indirect artillery fire support for their infantry divisions, usually as part of the divisional artillery effort. This was not the usual doctrinal role of tanks, but the practice began in the Mediterranean theater where tank battalions were often idle while on defensive missions. This was first officially accepted as a role for separate tank battalions in the November 1943 Training Circular No. 125. In reality, tank battalions in the ETO conducted little training for this role, particularly in terms of surveying and fire direction. As a result, when tank battalions were

assigned this mission, the divisional artillery usually had to perform these functions. Tank destroyer battalions, especially the towed battalions, were more commonly used in this role as their officers were usually drawn from the artillery branch and so were better trained for this mission.

Efforts were also undertaken to enhance the firepower of tanks in this role by designing artillery multiple rocket launchers such as the T34 4.5in. rocket launcher. This assembly mounted 60 rocket tubes over the turret of the tank and could deliver all the rockets in 30 seconds to a maximum range of 4,000 yards. The primary training group for this system was the 7th Armored Group. After rejecting the use of this device to support the D-Day landings, the first deployment in the ETO occurred in mid-December with the 743rd Tank Battalion in anticipation of a planned attack of the 30th Division. However, the German attack in the Ardennes led to the redeployment of the 30th Division to stop the 1st SS-Panzer Division, and as a result, the tanks jettisoned the launchers before using them. The T34 rocket launcher was subsequently used by a number of tank battalions. including the 712th, 753rd, and 781st Tank Battalions. For example, during the crossing of the Sauer and Our rivers by the 80th Division on February 7, 1945, one platoon of the 702nd Tank Battalion was fitted with the T34 to provide fire support, totaling 13 M4 tanks and a modified launcher on an M5A1 tank. An objective about 500 by 600ft in area was selected as the main target, and prisoners captured after the bombardment were shocked by its intensity. Although the infantry generally liked the concentrated effects of these rocket launchers, they were not popular with the tank battalions as they were clumsy and awkward to operate, and they distracted the tanks from their primary missions.

Tank destroyers, especially the towed tank destroyers, were used more often for indirect artillery fire support than tanks. Here, the 824th Tank Destroyer Battalion has their 3in. guns emplaced for artillery fire missions during February 1945. (MHI)

Lessons learned

The use of tanks to support the infantry divisions in the ETO proved to be highly successful. Indeed, the main complaint of infantry commanders was that there was never enough tank support. The centrality of tank support to US infantry tactics was emphasized in a captured German assessment of US infantry tactics: "Tanks are the main weapon of the [infantry] attack and are used in groups of up to 15 ... tank strong points containing up to 25 tanks form the backbone of the defense."

There was broad unanimity that the tank battalions had to be made organic to the divisions and not a separate organization in order to foster better knowledge of the use of tanks by infantry officers and to facilitate training and cooperation between tanks and infantry. The postwar General Board recommended abandoning the attachment of one separate tank battalion and one tank destroyer battalion to each infantry division, and instead to make a tank regiment organic to each division. This was a more sensible allocation since the three tank battalions in each regiment could be allotted to each infantry regiment, and each tank battalion could provide one tank company to each infantry battalion. The armored group concept was also abandoned as redundant.

The tank destroyer battalions

While the separate tank battalions quickly adapted to battlefield conditions in the ETO, the tank destroyer battalions were at the center of controversy for most of the campaign. At the time of the D-Day landings in Normandy, there were 30 tank destroyer battalions in England of which 11 were towed and 19 self-propelled. There was very little confidence in the tank destroyer doctrine of massing battalions to deal with the panzer threat, since the bocage presented such an obstacle to mobility that it seemed unlikely that battalions held in

An M3A1 halftrack of a towed tank destroyer battalion brings ashore its 3in. anti-tank gun at Utah Beach a few days after D-Day. The towed 3in. anti-tank guns proved unsuitable during the hedgerow fighting in Normandy but remained in service for the rest of 1944 in spite of frequent complaints. (NARA)

reserve in the rear could be rushed forward to meet a massed panzer attack. Furthermore, there were few massed panzer attacks in Normandy, yet there was a crying need for armored support by the infantry units that were having a rough time overcoming German defenses in the bocage. Almost from the outset, the battalions were attached to each infantry and armored division. The armored divisions invariably received self-propelled battalions while infantry divisions received the towed battalions and any leftover self-propelled battalions. The tactics of the self-propelled battalions evolved much along the same lines as the tank battalions described above.

Problems began to emerge almost immediately with the towed gun battalions. The 3in. gun was so heavy that it proved very difficult to move in the Normandy hedgerows. Once it was moved into position by its halftrack, the gun crews had a difficult time placing it into firing position due to the height of the hedgerows. Besides being clumsy to deploy, the 3in. gun was large and difficult to conceal, and crews were often subjected to small-arms and mortar fire, making their position untenable. During the hedgerow fighting, there were few occasions when the towed guns were used in their intended anti-tank role due to their shortcomings. Most of the fighting for the first two months of the campaign was a close-combat infantry struggle and the towed battalions had less to offer than the self-propelled battalions in such conditions. As a result, it became standard policy in most battalions of the First Army to take only two companies for anti-tank defense and leave one company behind the lines in the field artillery role. It was far from ideal in the artillery support role as its ammunition was tailored for anti-armor missions. Its high explosive round had only half the high explosive fill of a 75mm tank gun round, and only a fifth the high explosive of a 105mm howitzer round.

In comparison, the self-propelled M10 3in. GMC was more mobile in the bocage, and its armor gave the crew better protection. Infantry commanders

During the rapid advance across France and Belgium after the Operation Cobra breakout, tank destroyers were often used to speed the infantry assault by providing mobility to the assault companies. Here, the 3/22nd Infantry hitch a ride on an M10 3in. GMC of the 801st TD Battalion during operations near Mabompre, Belgium, on September 8, 1944. (NARA)

appreciated the psychological boost that the presence of the self-propelled tank destroyers gave their troops. Infantry divisions that received the self-propelled battalions usually committed a company of M10 tank destroyers with each rifle regiment, much as was the case with the tank battalions. The M10 was not ideally configured for the close-support role because its open roof left it vulnerable to sniper fire and close-range grenade attack. In addition, its armor was thinner than that of the M4 tank, and so it was more vulnerable to German anti-tank weapons. The lack of a power traverse for the turret was a significant drawback in close combat, as it took nearly 80 seconds to traverse the turret 180 degrees. The infantry preferred tank battalions to tank destroyer battalions for other reasons as well. A tank destroyer battalion had only 36 tank destroyers while a tank battalion had over 50 medium tanks and 17 light tanks, as well as six 105mm assault guns for added firepower. Regardless of these shortcomings, the M10 proved to be a very valuable and versatile vehicle when skilfully employed. A report by the commanding officer of the 5th Tank Destroyer Group in Normandy is illustrative of their successful role in the fighting:

What is not in the field manuals on tank destroyer use is the effective support which they render to a fighting infantry at the time of actual combat. An infantryman has his fortitude well tested and the mere presence of self-propelled tank destroyers in his immediate vicinity gives a tremendous shot of courage to the committed infantryman. For example, at Chambois [during the closing of the Falaise Gap in August 1944], an infantry battalion moved towards the town with utter fearlessness to enemy artillery, mortar, and small arms fire when accompanied by some M10s. However, the M10s were delayed in crossing a stream for about 35 minutes. During this time, the infantry battalion continued to their objective which dominated a roadway leading to Chambois. They fought infantry, they bazooka-ed some armored vehicles including three tanks on the road, but on realizing that the M10s weren't firing, they started a retirement. Leading the parade to the rear was a short lad known as "Shorty." Shorty in the lead was the first man to see a platoon of M10s who had finally gotten across the stream. Shorty took a good look at the M10s, turned around, and shouted to the other men "Hell boys, what are we retiring for, here comes the TDs!" The entire company in mass immediately reversed their direction and returned to their excellent positions, and to say they fought for the next few hours with unusual bravery is stating it mildly. The point I am trying to make is that the appearance and the knowledge that self-propelled tank destroyers were at hand was a major reason that the infantry attained success and victory. Often many men die or suffer to retain or exploit IF the inspiration furnished by the presence of self-propelled tank destroyers is known. The towed guns can be just as brave and thoroughly trained, but they never give much "oomph" to the fighting doughboy when the chips are really down.

The first massed panzer attack occurred on July 10, 1944, when the Panzer Lehr Division staged a counterattack near Isigny, attempting to drive a wedge through the American sector. It was the first large-scale encounter with the new Panther tank. By coincidence, the road used by the Panzer Lehr Division's Panther tank regiment near Le Desert ran through the sector covered by the 899th Tank Destroyer Battalion. As a result, there were a series of intense, close-range battles between the M10s and Panthers over a two-day period. Although the M10 had a great deal of difficulty penetrating the thick Panther frontal armor, the panzer was far more vulnerable on its flanks, and could be defeated by the 3in. gun at most combat ranges. In spite of the shortcomings of the 3in. gun, the 899th Tank Destroyer Battalion was credited with 12 Panthers, one

PzKpfw IV, and one StuG III, and played a central role in blunting the German attack. The tank destroyers took advantage of the hedgerow terrain, and much of the fighting took place at point-blank ranges of under 200m. The poor performance of the 3in. gun against the Panther in frontal engagement came as a shock to the tank destroyer crews, and a major controversy erupted over the lack of an adequate gun for dealing with the new threat.

The inadequate anti-tank capabilities of the M10 revealed by the Normandy tank fighting led to considerable pressure to field the new M36 tank destroyer with the 90mm gun as soon as possible, and on July 6, 1944, Eisenhower's HQ cabled back to the United States asking that all M10 battalions be converted to the M36 as soon as possible. Later tank fighting in August when the Germans launched a panzer counteroffensive near Mortain only reinforced the Normandy lessons. The First Army report noted that Mortain:

> demonstrated the superiority of the self-propelled battalion over the towed unit in conclusive fashion by sustaining fewer losses while destroying more enemy tanks. The mobility of the self-propelled weapon permitted a more flexible and resilient defense whereas the towed gun, once in position, was unable to maneuver against targets outside its narrow sector of fire or to escape when threatened of being overrun.

Tank and tank destroyer battalions in infantry divisions would sometimes be used in unison during assaults. Here an M4 provides overwatch as an M10 tank destroyer moves forward on October 20 during the final stage of the fighting in Aachen, Germany. (NARA)

73

A pair of M10 3in. GMCs of the 893rd Tank Destroyer Battalion move up a wooded road in the Hürtgen Forest on November 18, 1944, while supporting the 28th Division during this costly battle. (NARA)

As a result, in September 1944, Bradley's 12th Army Group requested that of the 52 tank destroyer battalions committed to the theater, 20 be converted to the promised M36 90mm GMC, 20 retain the existing M10 or M18, and the remaining 12 remain as towed battalions, but completely reequipped with the new T5E1 90mm anti-tank gun. In practice, the changes were slow to take effect since the M36 was slow in arriving in theater, and the towed 90mm gun never arrived in any significant quantities. The first 40 M36 tank destroyers arrived in France in the first week of September 1944 and were issued to the First US Army. After preparation and crew training, they first went into action in October 1944 during the fighting along the German border.

The autumn campaign along the Siegfried Line saw little use of panzers, so the tank destroyers saw little use in their planned role. The self-propelled M10 and M18 tank destroyers continued to be used in a close-support role not much different from tanks. Typical offensive missions were to follow the lead elements of the infantry, furnish flank protection during the advance, attack targets of opportunity during the advance, and establish an anti-tank defense once the objective was seized.

The towed battalions more often than not were used for secondary missions due to their lack of mobility and protection. For example, when the 30th Infantry Division was assigned to penetrate a sector of the Siegfried Line on

October 2, two companies from the attached towed 3in. tank destroyer battalion were assigned to support one of the infantry battalions making the initial attack. The standard tactics in most of the towed battalions during offensive action was to attempt to position two platoons on a hill in overwatch position as the infantry regiment advanced, and these platoons fired on the objective and against any German forces attempting to block the advance. The third platoon was left limbered up and would move forward once the objective was taken to create an anti-tank defense.

While tank battalions in the ETO were not used as often for indirect artillery fire as their counterparts in Italy, the artillery mission remained more important in the tank destroyer battalions in the ETO. Both towed and self-propelled battalions received specialized artillery fire direction and survey equipment in England before D-Day, and since many tank destroyer officers were from the artillery branch, there was generally more preparation to carry out these missions. Available theater stocks of high-explosive ammunition limited the extent of their use in this role, and the towed guns were more often used in this role than the self-propelled guns due to the greater demand for the self-propelled guns for direct infantry support.

The Ardennes campaign in December 1944 saw the tank destroyers put to their greatest test. Four US infantry divisions bore the brunt of the initial German attack, supported by several towed 3in. tank destroyer battalions. Losses in the 3in. towed battalions were brutally high, totaling 35 percent in December alone. The hapless 820th TD Battalion was assigned to the 14th Cavalry Group, thinly stretched across the Losheim Gap and at the center of the main German assault. The battalion was overrun in the first few days of fighting and lost 31 of its 36 guns. The neighboring 801st TD Battalion was assigned to the 99th Division and it lost 15 of its guns. In an interview after the tank fighting in Krinkelt–Rocherath, a 2nd Infantry Division officer emphatically stated that:

I want the self-propelled guns rather than the towed 3in. guns because the towed guns are too heavy and sluggish. You can't get them up to the front. My orders have been in almost every case to get the guns up to the front-line troops. I just couldn't do it in the daytime with the 3in. towed gun. I can get the 57s up pretty well, but you can always get self-propelled guns up better than towed ones.

The Ardennes doomed the towed battalions. The initial Ardennes fighting made it quite clear that the towed anti-tank gun battalions were extremely ineffective when fighting German armor on their own. One study concluded that the loss ratio in these circumstances was about 3:1 in favor of the attacking tanks. When integrated into an infantry defensive position, the towed anti-tank guns were barely adequate with an exchange ratio of 1:1.3 in favor of the guns. In contrast, the self-propelled M10 3in. tank destroyers had a favorable exchange ratio of 1:1.9 when operating on their own without infantry support and an excellent ratio of 1:6 when integrated into an infantry defense. The study noted that the towed 3in. guns were successful in only two out of nine defensive actions while the M10 tank destroyer battalions were successful in 14 of 16 defensive actions against German tanks. The First Army report noted that tank destroyer battalion losses totaled 119, of which 86 were towed guns, a remarkable disproportion that glaringly revealed the vulnerability of the towed guns. The report concluded "It is clear that during the battle of the Ardennes, the self-propelled battalion again proved its superiority over the towed battalion for both offensive and defensive action."

The army bureaucracy in Washington had been painfully slow to recognize the obvious deficiencies of the towed battalions, and so finally in January 1945, Bradley's 12th Army Group took matters into their own hands and began to convert all towed 3in. battalions to self-propelled battalions as soon as equipment

A grim reminder of the human cost of bad doctrine and poor equipment. A knocked-out 3in. gun in Honsfeld overrun by Kampfgruppe Peiper in the pre-dawn hours of December 17, 1944, during the start of the Ardennes offensive. Two companies from the 612th and 801st TD Battalions were stationed in the town, but were quickly brushed aside. (NARA)

became available. The 6th Army Group in Alsace later adopted the same policy after it learned similar lessons during the German Nordwind offensive in January 1945. Commanders especially wanted more of the M36 90mm GMC since this was the only tank destroyer that had a reasonably good chance of success against the Panther. But with shortages of M36s, and a surplus of unused M18 tank destroyers available, the M18 was used to reequip some battalions. Lingering shortages of new tank destroyers prevented the complete re-organization and when the war in Europe ended in May 1945, four battalions still had the towed 3in. guns compared to 41 with self-propelled tank destroyers. Of the 41 self-propelled battalions, 13 were equipped with the M18, and the rest were equipped with the M36 or a mixture of M10 and M36 tank destroyers.

The use of the self-propelled tank destroyer battalions in the concluding months of the war after the Battle of the Bulge followed much the same pattern as that of the tank battalions. The relative absence of German armor meant that the tank destroyers were usually used as a form of mobile close artillery support, with interludes of other missions including the support of divisional artillery. During the defense of the Remagen Bridge over the Rhine, a tank destroyer group was assigned to the mission to repulse an anticipated German counterattack. However, a massed panzer attack never came. During the rapid advances in the final month of the war, tank destroyer battalions were regularly

used to create mobile infantry–armor teams with the infantry riding on the tank destroyers to speed the assault.

The record of the tank destroyer battalions during the war in Europe was a good one, but due to the training and adaptability of the tank destroyer crews and not due to their inadequate equipment, flawed organization, and unrealistic tactical doctrine. Army opinion was that the tank destroyer concept had been a failure. Infantry division commanders after the war unanimously agreed that they would prefer to have the support of a tank battalion instead of a tank destroyer battalion. Tanks were better suited to close support tactics than the thinly armored tank destroyers, and the tank destroyers had consistently failed in their primary mission of defeating enemy tanks due to the late arrival of the M36 tank destroyer. As a result, the tank destroyer force was disbanded after the war, and the General Board recommended making a tank regiment organic to each infantry division.

A snow-camouflaged M10 of the 773rd TD Battalion near Benonchamps, Belgium, on January 21, 1945. This particular battalion was one of the highest scoring tank destroyer units in Europe with 103 German armored vehicles to its credit in January 1945. This particular vehicle was credited with five German tanks during a German counterattack near Oberwampach, Luxembourg, during the Battle of the Bulge. (NARA)

Unit status

Tank battalions

The **70th Tank Battalion** was the oldest and most experienced separate tank battalion in the ETO in 1944–45. It was originally a light tank battalion and served in combat in Tunisia in 1942–43, and again on Sicily in 1943. It was re-organized later in 1943 as a standard battalion. It was attached to the 4th Infantry Division for the Normandy landing on Utah Beach and received the Presidential Unit Citation for its performance. It continued to serve with the 4th Division, including the brutal fighting in the Hürtgen Forest in November 1944, and in the Ardennes in December 1944. It was briefly attached to the 83rd Division on July 17–18, 1944, and the 63rd Division on March 12–18, 1945. It ended the war with the 4th Division after crossing the Danube near the Austrian border on April 25, 1945.

The **191st Tank Battalion** was another senior battalion formed from four prewar National Guard tank companies. It landed in North Africa in 1943 but did not see any significant combat until the landings at Salerno in September 1943. It took part in the landings at Anzio in January 1944, and suffered heavy losses during the fighting on the approaches to Rome in the late spring of 1944. Like several Italian campaign veterans, it was assigned to the Seventh US Army

Unit insignia: tank destroyer battalion shoulder patch (upper right); 771st, 753rd, and 738th Tank Battalions. (Author)

landings in southern France for Operation Dragoon on August 15. It was attached for most of the 1944–45 campaign to the 45th Division: the exceptions were attachments to the 36th Division in late August 1944, to the 79th Division in December 1944, and to the 42nd Division in late February 1945. It took part in the fighting in the Vosges Mountains and in Alsace. During the Rhine crossing on March 25, 1945, it again used DD tanks. It took part in the capture of Nürnberg and Munich.

The **701st Tank Battalion** was originally organized as a special tank battalion with Leaflet night-fighting tanks, but was reorganized as a standard tank battalion in late October 1944. It was deployed with the Ninth Army in mid-December 1944 and attached to the 102nd Division for Operation Grenade in late February 1945. It was shifted to the 75th Division in late March 1945, and returned to the 102nd Division from April 4, 1945 to the end of the war, taking part in the crossing of the Weser River.

The **702nd Tank Battalion** entered combat with the 80th Division on August 8, 1944, and took part in the fighting around Argentan and, later, the Moselle River crossings in September. During the autumn, it supported the division in the fighting around Metz, and was deployed to Luxembourg City during the Ardennes fighting. It took part with the division in the Ourthe and Sauer river campaigns along the Siegfried Line in February 1945, but was briefly attached to the 76th Division for two weeks starting in March during the advance on Trier. It returned to the 80th Division, crossing the Rhine near Mainz on March 28 and ending the war near Regensburg.

The **707th Tank Battalion**, formerly 3/81st Armored of the 5th Armored Division, was originally deployed in England as part of the Ground Force Replacement System for training troops. However, the shortage of tanks was so great that it was sent to France and entered combat with the 28th Division on October 6, 1944, near Krinkelt, Belgium. It served with the division during the savage fighting in the Hürtgen Forest in November losing most of its tanks, and was again decimated in December 1944, while supporting the 28th Division in its costly defense of the approaches to Bastogne during the Battle of the Bulge. Reconstituted companies were briefly attached to the 17th Airborne Division during the final phase of the Ardennes fighting in mid-January and the rebuilt battalion had a succession of attachments in April 1945, starting with the 76th Division on April 2, the 65th Division on April 6, and the 89th Division.

The **709th Tank Battalion**, formerly the 3/40th Armored, 7th Armored Division, entered combat with the 8th Infantry Division on July 13, 1944, and fought in the Normandy and Brittany campaigns. Elements of the battalion fought alongside the 83rd Division during the fighting for the Breton ports. It was deployed in Luxembourg for most of October, re-entering combat with the 8th Infantry Division in the Hürtgen Forest on November 19. It was transferred to the 78th Division on December 10, taking part in the fighting for the Siegfried Line near the Monschau Corridor. It was transferred to the 75th Division on January 31, 1945, during the fighting for the Colmar Pocket in Alsace, then to the 95th Division on 16 February for the fighting in the Ruhr.

The **712th Tank Battalion**, formerly the 3/11th Armored, 10th Armored Division, served in combat alongside the 90th Division from June 28, 1944, and took part in the liberation of Le Mans. It helped to defeat an attack by Panzer Brigade 106 near Landres that was a prelude to the panzer counteroffensive against Patton's Third Army in Lorraine. It remained in Lorraine through the autumn during the fighting around Metz, and took part in the final actions in the Battle of the Bulge in late January 1945. It took part in the fighting along the German frontier with the 90th Division in February, and ended the war in Czechoslovakia.

The **717th Tank Battalion** was assigned to the Armored Board at Ft. Knox for testing new equipment including the new T26E3 heavy tank. It was sent to Europe in late 1944 and entered combat with the 79th Division on March 8,

An M4 of the 709th Tank Battalion uses the shelter of a shattered house in the devastated town of Hürtgen on December 5 after the town was taken by the 121st Infantry, 8th Division. The M4 is still fitted with a Rhino hedgerow cutter. In the foreground is a burned-out M4 tank lost in the earlier fighting on November 28. (NARA)

1945, remaining with it during the rest of the war except for a two-day assignment with the 75th Division in mid-April and a brief attachment to the 17th Airborne Division for the attack on Essen.

The **735th Tank Battalion** entered combat in Normandy on July 13, 1944, alongside the 5th Infantry Division and served with it in the race across France and the fighting near Metz, including the ill-fated assault on Ft. Driant. After being reequipped, it was transferred to the 95th Division on October 20, until returning to the 5th Division in late November for the final clean-up operations around Metz. It relieved the 778th Tank Battalion in defensive positions along the Saar River in mid-December 1944, and on December 21 was transferred to the 26th Division for the fighting in the Ardennes until the end of January 1945. On February 1 it was attached to the 87th Division for the push against the Siegfried Line, and served with this division for most of the remaining months of the war, including the Rhine crossing on March 25, 1945.

The **736th Tank Battalion** was another of the special battalions with the Leaflet tank and was reorganized in November 1944, before being attached to the 94th Division laying siege to the encircled Breton ports. It entered combat alongside the 76th Division on January 25, 1945, remaining with it until the beginning of February. On February 5, it was attached to the 83rd Division, remaining with it until the end of the war. During the Rhine crossing, one of its companies was equipped with DD tanks.

The **737th Tank Battalion** entered combat alongside the 35th Division on July 9, 1944, in Normandy, serving with it for most of the summer and autumn campaign. It was the first Third Army tank battalion over the Moselle River and remained in combat in Lorraine for the remainder of the autumn fighting. It was transferred to the 5th Infantry Division on December 23 during the

Ardennes campaign, taking part in the capture of Bitburg. It remained with the 5th Infantry Division until the end of the war, ending up with Patton's Third Army in Czechoslovakia.

The **738th Tank Battalion (SMX)** was one of two special Leaflet tank battalions converted to Special Mine Exploder (SMX) configuration in October 1944. It was attached to the First US Army and spent the remainder of the war on a variety of specialized missions.

The **739th Tank Battalion (SMX)** was the second of two special Leaflet tank battalions converted to Special Mine Exploder battalions in October 1944. It was attached to the Ninth Army. During the Roer River operation in February 1945, some of its personnel operated LVT amphibious tractors, and one of its platoons was reequipped with M4 Crocodiles and attached to the 29th Division's 175th Infantry for the assault on the fortified citadel in Jülich on February 24, 1945. This battalion was the Ninth Army's specialist armored formation, and in March had one company equipped with DD tanks for the Rhine crossing, and another company with CDL Leaflet tanks for protecting the crossings.

The **740th Tank Battalion** was one of the special tank battalions equipped with the Leaflet night-fighting tank. When reconfigured as a standard tank battalion, its troops were dispatched to Belgium as reinforcements during the Battle of the Bulge. Arriving in Belgium with no tanks of its own, the unit was instructed to scrape up whatever tanks it could find and it ended up with a hodge-podge of types. The battalion entered combat alongside the 30th Division during the fighting against Kampfgruppe Peiper near La Gleize, remaining with the division until late December when it was transferred to the 82nd Airborne Division. On February 6, 1945, it was attached to the 8th Division, remaining with it for most of the rest of the war except for short attachments to the 70th Division and the 63rd Division in mid-March 1945, during the fighting along the Siegfried Line.

The **741st Tank Battalion** was attached to the 1st Infantry Division for the D-Day landings on Omaha beach. The battalion lost nearly all of its tanks on D-Day and was reequipped, subsequently being attached to the 2nd Infantry Division for the remainder of the Normandy campaign, the autumn fighting along the Siegfried Line, and the defense of Krinkelt–Rocherath in the opening phase of the Battle of the Bulge. It subsequently took part in the fighting along the German frontier, reaching the Rhine River in March, and ended the war in Czechoslovakia.

The **743rd Tank Battalion** landed in support of the 116th Regimental Combat Team at Omaha Beach on D-Day and was decorated with the Presidential Unit Citation for its actions. After refitting, it was transferred to the 30th Division, and fought alongside it during the Normandy campaign, the defense of Mortain against the German panzer counter-offensive, the advance into Belgium and the autumn campaign along the Siegfried Line. It was part of the force that stopped Kampfgruppe Peiper, the spearhead of the Sixth Panzer Army in the Ardennes. It took part in Operation Grenade, crossing the Roer in late February, and crossed the Rhine in late March with an attached DD tank company from the 736th Tank Battalion. It ended the war in Magdeburg, Germany.

The **744th Tank Battalion (Light)** was first deployed in Normandy with the 28th Division in late July for the Normandy breakout and the race to the Seine. Due to its light tank configuration, it was then attached to the 113th Cavalry Group for much of the

Some tank battalions had the good fortune of remaining attached to a single infantry division for most of the fighting, such as the 741st Tank Battalion and the 2nd Infantry Division. Here, troops of the division's 9th Infantry Regiment mount an M4A1 (76mm) near Schöneseiffen, Germany, on February 2, 1945, following the Battle of the Bulge. (NARA)

autumn of 1944 fighting along the Siegfried Line, with short attachments to the 29th Division in October 1944, and the 102nd Division in December. It was attached to the 30th Division in February for Operation Grenade, the Roer River crossing, and was then attached to the 75th Division in March for the remaining fighting in Germany.

The **745th Tank Battalion** was attached to the 1st Infantry Division for D-Day, landing one company in the later waves on June 6. It remained with the "Big Red One" for the remainder of the campaign in Europe including the St. Lô breakout, the fighting for Aachen, and Operation Queen in November 1944. It took part in the fighting in the Ardennes on the northern shoulder, as well as the later advance through the Siegfried Line, and the Ruhr valley encirclement. It ended the war in Czechoslovakia.

The **746th Tank Battalion** was part of the second wave of units landing at Utah beach on D-Day. It was first committed to action with the ill-starred 90th Division on June 12 but was quickly transferred to the experienced 9th Infantry Division, which advanced on the port of Cherbourg. It took part in the race to the Seine and the advance into Belgium, and served with the division during the bloody fighting in the Hürtgen Forest. It took part in the fighting for the Roer River in January 1945, was the first separate tank battalion over the Remagen Bridge after elements of the 9th Armored Division, and ended the war near the Mulde River.

The **747th Tank Battalion** landed on Omaha Beach on D+1 and was attached to the 29th Division during the fighting in Normandy, the race across France, the advance into Belgium, and the fighting along the Siegfried Line. The battalion supported the 29th Division in the fighting towards the Roer River in November 1944–February 1945. In March the battalion was trained to operate LVT amphibious tractors and used these to support the crossing by the 30th Division on March 24, 1945. One tank company took part in the Ruhr encirclement and the battalion ended up in Germany at the end of the war.

The **748th Tank Battalion** was one of the special Leaflet night-fighting tank battalions that was converted to a standard tank battalion in October 1944. It was first deployed in late January 1945 with the 94th Division and fought along the Siegfried Line. It was withdrawn for a few weeks in early March to retrain on CDL Leaflet tanks and DD amphibious tanks, and was used to support the Rhine crossing by the 5th Infantry Division on March 23, 1945. It had two companies of CDL Leaflet tanks that were used to protect Rhine River crossings, and to assist engineer units in night construction projects with Patton's Third Army. It turned in its specialized tanks and was attached to the 65th Division in early April, taking part in the advance in southern Germany and ending the war in Austria near Linz.

The **749th Tank Battalion** was attached to the 79th Division in late June 1944 and took part in the Normandy campaign and the race for the Seine, being one of the first tank units across the river in August. It was subsequently transferred to the Seventh Army in Alsace and first deployed with the 44th Division on October 23, 1944, for the fighting near Mutzig along the old Maginot Line. It fought along the German frontier with the division during the January Operation Nordwind attack, and, starting in February, it supported the 70th, 71st, and 42nd Divisions for short operations until attached to the 76th Division in early April where it remained until the end of the war.

The **750th Tank Battalion** deployed with the 104th Division near Aachen in October 1944 and went into combat on November 16, 1944, along the Siegfried Line during the fighting on the approaches to the Roer River. It was attached to the 75th Division in the Ardennes from mid-December 1944 to the end of January 1945. It returned to the 104th Division, took part in Operation Grenade in February 1945, and met up with Red Army troops on the Mulde River on April 21, 1945.

The **753rd Tank Battalion** was one of the most experienced tank battalions in the US Army in 1944, having served in the North Africa, Sicily, and Italy campaigns. It landed in southern France with the 36th Division on August 15, 1944, as part of Operation Dragoon and remained with the division for most of the subsequent fighting including the Vosges campaign, the liberation of Strasbourg, and Operation Nordwind in January 1945. After serving briefly under corps control during the Rhine crossing, it was transferred to the 63rd Division at the end of March 1945, and ended up in Austria at the end of the war.

The **756th Tank Battalion** was another long-serving unit with experience in North Africa and Italy before being attached to the 3rd Infantry Division for the invasion of southern France in August 1944 with DD tanks. The battalion took part in the advance to the Belfort Gap, the fighting for the Vosges Mountains and the liberation of Strasbourg. During the crossing of the Rhine near Worms on March 26, one of its companies employed DD tanks again. Although normally attached to the 3rd Infantry Division, it had a short assignment with the 103rd Division in March 1945 and after returning to the 3rd, was part of the spearhead that seized Berchtesgarden and Salzburg in May 1945.

The **759th Tank Battalion (Light)** was committed to support the 2nd Infantry Division on June 18, 1944, in Normandy, and also later supported the 101st Airborne in late June and early July policing up German stragglers on the Cherbourg peninsula. Due to its configuration, it spent most of the war attached to the 4th Cavalry Group, starting with the advance past Chartres and the race towards Belgium. It crossed the Rhine in early March and ended the war near Ascherleben.

A GI of the 94th Division walks through a gap in a roadblock in Lampaden past an M4A3 (76mm) of the 778th Tank Battalion that has been knocked out by two gun penetrations through the transmission cover during the fighting for the Saarbrucken bridgehead on March 9, 1945. (NARA)

The **761st Tank Battalion (Colored)** was the most decorated African-American armored unit of the war, first being committed to support the 26th Division in late October 1944, and subsequently the 87th Division in mid-December, the 17th Airborne Division in the concluding weeks of the Ardennes fighting in late January 1945, the 95th Division in early February, the 79th Division in late February, the 103rd Division in early March 1945, and the 71st Division from late March until the end of the war. It met up with the Red Army on May 5 near Steyr, Austria. It was awarded the Presidential Unit Citation in 1975.

The **771st Tank Battalion** was spun off from the reorganization of the 4th Armored Division in 1943 and was first committed to action in support of the 102nd Division in late November during the fighting towards the Roer River. It was transferred to the 84th Division in mid-December 1944 during the Battle of the Bulge and remained with the division through most of the rest of the war, except for an interlude in mid-March 1945 when it supported the 17th Airborne Division during the Rhine River operation.

The **772nd Tank Battalion** didn't reach Europe until February 1945 and was attached to the 44th Division from late March until the end of the war, taking part in the attack on Mannheim, and ending the war in Austria.

The **774th Tank Battalion** was first deployed with the 83rd Division at the end of August 1944, and took part in the drive to the Seine and into Lorraine. It supported the 83rd Division during the final phase of the fighting in the Hürtgen Forest in December 1944, and took part in the counterattack phase of the Battle of the Bulge. It was transferred to the 76th Division on February 3, 1945, and took part in the capture of the Roer dams. The battalion briefly supported the 101st Airborne Division in the final days of the war in May 1945 during the seizure of Berchtesgaden.

The **777th Tank Battalion**, formerly the 1/3rd Armored, 10th Armored Division, later served as a test unit at Ft. Knox. It was first committed with the 28th Division at the end of February 1945 and subsequently supported the 69th Division from the end of March to the conclusion of the war including the liberation of Colditz prison and the capture of Leipzig.

The **778th Tank Battalion** was first committed to support the 95th Division in mid-November 1944 during the final fighting for the fortress city of Metz and remained with the division during the fierce fighting for Saarlautern. The battalion was transferred to support the 26th Division on January 29, 1945, except for some short assignments to the 94th Division in February and March along the Siegfried Line. It was advancing on Prague, Czechoslovakia, when the war ended.

The **781st Tank Battalion** was first committed to support the 100th Division in early December 1944 during the fighting in Alsace and remained with the division for most of the war except for assignments to the 70th Division in early January 1945 and the 103rd Division for two weeks in late January 1945 during Operation Nordwind. It was subsequently reassigned to the 100th Division and was involved in the capture of Bitche, and the Rhine crossing on March 31. The battalion ended the war in Austria near Innsbruck, though one company served with the 103rd Division near the Brenner Pass at this time.

The **782nd Tank Battalion** arrived in Germany in the final few weeks of the war, supporting the 97th Division in late April and early May 1945 and ending the war in Czechoslovakia.

The **784th Tank Battalion (Colored)** was deployed with the 104th Division at the end of December 1944 in the Roer sector and transferred to the 35th Division at the beginning of February 1945 for Operation Grenade, serving with the unit until the end of the war, including the Rhine crossing on March 26, and the battle for the Ruhr pocket.

The **786th Tank Battalion**, formerly 1/47th Armored, 14th Armored Division, arrived in theater on February 23, 1945, and was attached to the 99th Division. It crossed the Rhine on March 10 at Remagen and took part in the final operations around the Ruhr pocket, ending the war near Landshut, Germany.

The **787th Tank Battalion**, formerly the 3/16th Armored, 16th Armored Division, arrived only on May 2, 1945, and supported the 86th Division for the last few days of the war without any combat with the Wehrmacht.

Tank destroyer battalions

The **601st TD Battalion** first saw combat in North Africa and later on Sicily and in Italy. During the campaign in France, it was attached to the 3rd Infantry Division, which took part in the landings in southern France in August 1944, equipped with the M10 3in. GMC. It served with the division until the end of the war and was the longest-serving tank destroyer battalion of the US Army in World War II. It was completely reequipped with the M36 by January 1945.

The **602nd TD Battalion**, equipped with M18 76mm GMC, first deployed with the 26th Division on October 23, 1944, during the fighting in the Saar. During the Battle of the Bulge, it was first deployed with the 28th Division during the fighting on the approaches to Bastogne, and at the end of the month was shifted to the newly arrived 11th Armored Division. It remained with the 11th Armored Division until March when it was transferred to the 89th Division, remaining with it until the end of the war.

The **603rd TD Battalion**, equipped with M18 76mm GMC, first entered combat in late July with the 6th Armored Division during Operation Cobra, the breakout from Normandy. It remained with the division until the end of the war, and was the highest-scoring M18 battalion in the ETO.

The **605th TD Battalion** was equipped with towed 3in. anti-tank guns and first deployed with the 102nd Division on February 15, 1945, in preparation for Operation Grenade, the assault over the Roer. It was transferred to the 84th Division for the first week of March. During the last week of April 1944 it served with the 79th Division and 82nd Airborne Division, ending the war attached to the 82nd Airborne Division.

The 744th Tank Battalion was the only separate battalion completely reequipped with the M24 light tank and one is seen here to the left following a skirmish between Task Force Hunt and the 116th Panzer Division near Kirchhellen on March 25, 1945. An M10 from the 823rd Tank Destroyer Battalion, also supporting the 30th Division, is evident in the center, and to the right is a smoldering SdKfz 251/21 knocked out during the fighting. (USMA)

A column from Company A, 801st TD Battalion, passes through Montebourg, France, on June 21, 1944, with an M20 armored car in the lead followed by an M3 halftrack towing a 3in. anti-tank gun. (MHI)

The **607th TD Battalion** deployed with the 90th Division in Normandy in late June with the towed 3in. anti-tank gun and remained with the division through the end of November when it was converted to a self-propelled battalion. It was attached to the 87th Division in early February and remained with the division for most of the remainder of the campaign in Europe, ending the war equipped with M36 90mm GMC.

The **609th TD Battalion** was equipped with the M18 76mm GMC and deployed with the 10th Armored Division on October 16, 1944, remaining with the division through the war.

The **610th TD Battalion** was converted from towed to self-propelled with the new M36 in October 1944 prior to being committed to combat. It was first deployed with the 26th Division on November 12, remaining with it for a month during the fighting in the Saar. It served with the 87th Division during the middle of December 1944, and was attached to the 4th Infantry Division from the end of January through May, except for a few days in mid-March when it supported the 42nd Division. It ended the war equipped with M36 90mm GMC.

The **612th TD Battalion** was initially deployed as a towed battalion with the 2nd Infantry Division and served with it from mid-June 1944 until the end of the war. It was reequipped with the M18 76mm GMC at the end of December 1944 due to heavy losses in the Ardennes.

The **614th TD Battalion (Colored)** was first attached to the 95th Division in late November during the fighting for the Saar, and was attached to the 103rd Division during the final few weeks of the war in Europe. It remained a towed battalion for the duration of the fighting.

The **628th TD Battalion** first deployed with the 5th Armored Division on August 2, 1944, during the race across France and remained with the division for most of the European campaign except for the Battle of the Bulge. The battalion was attached to the 78th Division on December 19–23, and the 82nd Airborne Division on January 2–11, 1945, returning to the 5th Armored Division at the end of the month. It ended the war with M36 90mm GMC.

The **629th TD Battalion** deployed with the 9th Infantry Division in France during the third week of August, and then served with the 28th Division, during the last two weeks of September during the Siegfried Line fighting and the 2nd Infantry Division during November. During the Battle of the Bulge it supported the 75th Division until early January when it was attached to the 83rd Division. It served with the 82nd Airborne Division during the first two weeks of February, and the 99th Division from the last week of February until the end of the war, concluding the campaign equipped with the M36 90mm GMC.

The **630th TD Battalion** was a towed battalion and supported the 28th Division from July 20, 1944, until the end of the campaign, except for a few days in mid-April when elements were attached to the 97th Division. As such it was involved in some of the most intense combat of the war including the Siegfried Line campaign, the bloody Hürtgen Forest fighting, and the opening phase of the Ardennes offensive. It was reequipped with the M36 by the end of the campaign.

The **633rd TD Battalion**, equipped with the M18 76mm GMC, entered the war at the beginning of May 1945, and served with the 16th Armored Division for only a few days before the conflict ended.

The **634th TD Battalion**, equipped with M10 3in. GMC, served with the 1st Infantry Division from the beginning of August 1944 until the end of the war in Europe, seeing fighting in most of the major engagements of the war including the Normandy battles and the Battle of the Bulge.

The **635th TD Battalion** was a towed battalion deployed with the 1st Infantry Division in Normandy from June 7 until the end of September, and later served with the 71st Division from mid-March 1945 until the end of the war. It was one of a handful of battalions that retained the towed configuration through the campaign.

The **636th TD Battalion** deployed with the 36th Division and remained with the division until the end of the war, except for some short interludes when elements of the battalion supported the 45th Division in October 1944, and the 13th Armored Division during late March and April 1945.

The **638th TD Battalion**, equipped with the M18 76mm GMC, deployed with the 84th Division at the beginning of December 1944, and took part in the subsequent Ardennes fighting. It remained with the division until the end of the war.

The **643rd TD Battalion**, equipped with M18 76mm GMC, first supported the 82nd Airborne Division in early January 1945 in the Ardennes and then served with the 83rd Division from the beginning of February until the end of the war.

The **644th TD Battalion**, equipped with the M10 3in. GMC, served with the 8th Infantry Division from July 1944 until the end of the war, except for interludes when elements of the battalion supported the 2nd Infantry Division in the Ardennes from December 12, 1944, to January 27, 1945, and the 99th Division from January 28 to February 8, 1945.

The **645th TD Battalion** served during the North Africa and Sicily campaigns, and deployed from Italy with the 45th Division in southern France, serving with it until the end of March 1945, except for a few weeks with the 42nd Division in late February and a few days in late March with the 75th Division. It began with the M10, but was completely reequipped with the M36 by January 1945.

The **648th TD Battalion** served with the 70th Division from February 20, 1945, until the end of March and in April 1945 supported the 86th Division. It did not convert from towed to self-propelled until after the end of the war.

The **654th TD Battalion** supported the 35th Division for most of the fighting in Europe, except for December 22–25 when it supported the 5th Infantry

Division. It was initially equipped with the M10 3in. GMC and subsequently with the M36.

The **656th TD Battalion** first deployed with the 9th Armored Division on February 22, 1945, and remained with the division until the end of the war. It was initially equipped with the M18, and was later reequipped with the M36 90mm GMC.

The **661st TD Battalion**, equipped with M18 76mm GMC, first deployed with the 69th Division on February 7, 1945, and remained with the unit through the end of the war.

The **679th TD Battalion (Colored)** deployed to France as a towed AT gun battalion and arrived in Europe in late January 1945. It saw little combat and was redeployed to Italy in late February 1945.

The **691st TD Battalion** was deployed as a towed AT gun battalion. It first supported the 35th Division on September 5–9, 1944, the 80th Division on September 16–18, and the 26th Division from mid-October until early December 1944. During the Battle of the Bulge it was attached to the 6th Armored Division during the middle of December, and then to the 87th Division at the end of the month. It served with the 76th Division from late January through February 1945, the 65th Division through most of March and was partly reequipped in one company with the M36 90mm GMC at the end of March 1945. It was subsequently attached to the 76th Division from early April until the end of the war. Elements of the battalion supported the 8th Armored Division at various times from early February to May 1945.

The **692nd TD Battalion** entered combat with the 104th Division on October 29, 1944, during the Siegfried Line campaign as a towed AT gun unit and

An M36 90mm gun motor carriage of the 703rd Tank Destroyer Battalion, 3rd Armored Division, passes by a knocked-out PzKpfw IV of 15th Pz.Gren. Div. near Langlir on January 13, 1945. (NARA)

remained with the division until early March 1945. It served for most of the remainder of the war with the 42nd Division and converted to the self-propelled M36 GMC in early February 1945.

The **702nd TD Battalion** spent most of the European campaign attached to the 2nd Armored Division originally with the M10 3in. GMC and later with the M36 90mm GMC.

The **703rd TD Battalion** spent most of the campaign in Europe with the 3rd Armored Division except for a brief interlude during the Battle of the Bulge when it was attached to the 1st Infantry Division in the fighting along Elsenborn Ridge. It was originally equipped with the M10 3in. GMC and reequipped with the M36 90mm GMC by the end of the campaign.

The **704th TD Battalion** was one of the first M18 battalions to see service and it entered combat with the 4th Armored Division during Operation Cobra in July 1944. It remained with the 4th Armored Division, except for some brief attachments to the 87th Division in mid-December 1944 and the 94th Division in January–March 1945. It received a handful of M36s shortly before the end of the war.

The **705th TD Battalion** was equipped with M18 76mm GMC and first supported the 95th Division in mid-October 1944. During the Battle of the Bulge, it supported the 101st Airborne Division during the defense of Bastogne, and became famous for its efforts in defeating the attacks of the German 15th Pz.Gren. Div. over Christmas. In late February, it was attached to the 11th Armored Division and remained with it until the end of the war. It received a handful of M36s shortly before the end of the war.

The **771st TD Battalion** supported the 77th Division in late September 1944, and was attached to the 102nd Division from early November for most of the rest of the war aside from some interludes with the 11th Cavalry Group. It was originally equipped with the M10 3in. GMC and later with the M36 90mm GMC.

The **772nd TD Battalion** was a towed 3in. AT gun unit and deployed in support of the 83rd Division on December 22 during the Battle of the Bulge, until being transferred to the 75th Division where it remained for most of the rest of the war. It was reequipped with the M36 by the end of the campaign.

The **773rd TD Battalion**, equipped with M10 3in. GMC, supported the 79th Division starting in early September 1944 during the fighting on the French–Belgian border, the 95th Division starting in late October 1944, and finally the 90th Division from the beginning of November until the end of the war. It retained the M10 through the campaign, but received a handful of M36s shortly before the end of the war.

The **774th TD Battalion** was a towed AT gun unit and supported the 5th Infantry Division starting in mid-September 1944 near Metz, the 95th Division in late October, and then returned to support the 5th Infantry Division for most of November. During the fighting in the Ardennes, it supported the 90th Division from December 21 until early January and then was attached to the 94th Division from early January until the end of the war. It was reequipped with the M36 90mm GMC in late January 1945.

The **776th TD Battalion** served in North Africa and Italy, and was shipped to France in October 1944. It supported the 44th Division from November along the Maginot Line through the end of the war, except for some attachments to the 63rd Division in late March 1945 and the 4th Infantry Division in mid-April. It was originally equipped with the M10 3in. GMC and was reequipped with the M36 90mm GMC by November 1944.

The **801st TD Battalion** equipped with the towed 3in. gun, supported the 4th Infantry Division from June 13 through early November, the 99th Division until early February, the 30th Division in late February and the 83rd Division through mid-April 1945. It was partly reequipped with the M18 76mm GMC in late March 1945 while in the Harz Mountains.

The **802nd TD Battalion** began as a towed AT gun unit and deployed with the 83rd Division in Normandy in early July 1944, remaining in support of the unit until early December. It supported the 4th Infantry Division on the southern shoulder of the Ardennes front through Christmas. It was attached to the 80th Division in late January and the 95th Division in early February, remaining with the 95th through most of the rest of the fighting. It was reequipped with the M36 90mm GMC in early March 1945.

The **803rd TD Battalion** served with the 3rd Armored Division during the Normandy fighting in June and July 1944, before deploying for a few weeks with the troubled 90th Division in early July and the 28th Division in late July 1944. It supported the 4th Infantry Division on the southern Ardennes front from early November until Christmas, and was attached to the 5th Infantry Division from Christmas until the end of the war. It was originally equipped with the M10 3in. GMC and later with the M36 90mm GMC.

The **807th TD Battalion** was a towed AT gun unit and first supported the 83rd Division in late September and early October 1944. It was attached to the 5th Division in early December and the 90th Division in late December 1944 during the Ardennes fighting. The battalion was deployed with the 101st Airborne Division for a month starting in late January 1945, and was then deployed in a succession of short assignments with the 35th Division in early March, the 30th and 75th Divisions in late March, and the 86th Division from

An M36 90mm GMC with infantry tank riders aboard during the fighting near St. Vith, Belgium, on January 23, 1945, during the concluding phase of the Battle of the Bulge. (NARA)

late April until the end of the war. It began receiving the M18 shortly before the end of the campaign but was not fully reequipped.

The **808th TD Battalion** served with the 80th Division from late September through Christmas in a towed AT gun configuration. It converted to M36 90mm GMC in late January 1945. It supported the 76th Division during March 1945 and was attached to the 65th Division from April 5 until the end of the war.

The **809th TD Battalion** was equipped with M18 76mm GMC and served from February 9 until the end of the war with the 8th Armored Division, except for some assignments with the 79th Division in late March and the 95th Division in early April. It received a small number of M36s towards the end of the campaign.

The **811th TD Battalion** was equipped with the M18 76mm GMC and first deployed with the 9th Armored Division in November 1944. It served with the division during the Battle of the Bulge and was transferred to support the 17th Airborne Division during the final two weeks of fighting in the Ardennes in January 1945. It was subsequently attached to the 11th Armored Division in early February before being attached to the 80th Division where it remained for most of the rest of the war.

The **813th TD Battalion** served in North Africa and first deployed with the 79th Division in Normandy on July 1, 1944, remaining with the division for most of the war, except for assignments to the 44th Division in the last week of October 1944, and the 101st Airborne Division in the last few days of the war in May 1945. It was originally equipped with the M10 3in. GMC and later with the M36 90mm GMC.

The **814th TD Battalion** served with the 7th Armored Division starting in mid-August 1944 and remained with it, except for some short assignments to the 75th Division in the first week of January 1945 and the 99th Division in the second week of February 1945. It was originally equipped with the M10 3in. GMC and later with the M36 90mm GMC.

The **817th TD Battalion** was equipped with the M18 76mm GMC and first deployed with the 78th Division in early December 1944 along the Siegfried Line. It supported the 8th Infantry Division for most of December 1944 through early February, and subsequently the 99th Division in late February and the 104th Division in April and May 1945.

The **818th TD Battalion** deployed with the 5th Infantry Division on July 13 and remained with the division until late December, when it was attached to the 26th Division for the duration of the war. It was originally equipped with the M10 3in. GMC and later with the M36 90mm GMC.

The **820th TD Battalion** was a towed 3in. AT gun unit and deployed with the ill-fated 106th Division that was overrun in the opening phase of the Battle of the Bulge near St. Vith. Surviving elements of the battalion retreated with the 7th Armored Division and served in the later fighting against the 2nd SS-Panzer Corps. It was reequipped with M18 tank destroyers in March 1945. The battalion was attached to the 97th Division in late April and remained with it until the end of the war a few weeks later.

The **821st TD Battalion** deployed in Normandy as a towed AT gun unit and supported the 35th Division in the July fighting. The battalion was reorganized as a self-propelled battalion in late December 1944 with the M10.

The **822nd TD Battalion** was equipped with towed AT guns and first deployed with the 63rd Division on February 6, 1945, along the Saar River. It served with the division until the end of the war. It was reequipped with the M18 76mm GMC in mid-April 1945.

The **823rd TD Battalion** was equipped with towed 3in. anti-tank guns and first deployed in support of the 30th Division in late June, fighting in support of the division in the critical battles including the defense of Mortain in July 1944. The battalion was reorganized with the M10 3in. GMC in mid-December 1944.

Infantry from the 30th Infantry Division mount up on an M10 3in. GMC of the 823rd Tank Destroyer Battalion during preparations for crossing the Rhine River in the Ninth Army sector on March 24, 1945. The main push over the Rhine began the following day. (NARA)

The **824th TD Battalion** deployed with the 100th Division as a towed unit on November 26 during the Vosges fighting and remained with it until late April. It was reequipped with the M18 76mm GMC in mid-March 1944. It was attached to the 103rd Division on April 24, remaining with it for the last two weeks of the war.

The **827th TD Battalion (Colored)** converted from towed AT guns to M18 76mm GMC in July 1944 before being deployed to France in November 1944. The unit was poorly trained and, after poor performance during the fighting in Hatten-Rittershoffen in Alsace, it was withdrawn in mid-February 1945.

The **893rd TD Battalion**, equipped with the M10 3in. GMC, served with the 4th Infantry Division starting on August 23, 1944. In late October it supported the 28th Division during the opening phase of the Hürtgen Forest fighting, and was attached to the 78th Division from December 11, 1944, until the end of the war. It retained the M10 tank destroyer until the end of the war.

The **899th TD Battalion** was first deployed with the 9th Infantry Division on June 19, 1944, in Normandy and supported the division through late July. It was originally equipped with the M10 3in. GMC and later with the M36 90mm GMC.

Bibliography

There is extensive documentation on the tank and tank destroyer battalions, though much of it is scattered and difficult to find except at specialized military libraries such as the Military History Institute (MHI) at the Army War College at Carlisle Barracks, Pennsylvania. Many of the battalions published short histories after the war, but these tend to be difficult to find as they were often self-published. A few of the histories recently published by regular publishing firms are listed below. Preserved unit records of the battalions vary enormously in depth and quality, and can be found in RG 407 at the National Archives and Records Administration in College Park, MD. There are numerous reports preserved in the archives dealing with the lessons learned by tank and tank destroyer battalions during the war. The US Army Ground Forces *Reports of Observers—ETO 1944–45* contains hundreds of reports dealing with the combat experiences of these units, and a collated edition can be found at MHI. The senior commands of the Army also compiled histories after the war, and some of the most useful include the *First US Army Report of Operations* and Vol. XI of the *12th Army Group Report of Operations—Final After Action Report*. For readers looking for a more detailed look at the combat experiences of US tankers in the ETO, one of the best accounts is a thinly fictionalized account by a veteran of the 743rd Tank Battalion, Wayne Robinson's *Barbara, A Novel of Death and Survival in Tank Combat* (Doubleday, 1962). A more detailed look at the equipment used in the tank and tank destroyer battalions is provided in the Osprey New Vanguard series including the M5A1 light tank (NVG 33); M4 (76mm) medium tank (NVG 73); M10 and M36 tank destroyer (NVG 57); M18 tank destroyer (NVG 97); and towed anti-tank guns (NVG 107).

US Army studies

A Critical Analysis of the History of Armor in World War II, Armored School, Ft. Knox (April 1953)

Armored Action in WWII: Use of Armor in Defense, Armored School, Ft. Knox (May 1950)

Armored Special Equipment, General Board, US Forces, European Theater (Study No. 52)

Armor in Night Attack, Armored School, Ft. Knox (June 1950)

Armor in the Attack of Fortified Positions, Armored School, Ft. Knox (May 1950)

Armor in Winter Warfare, Armored School, Ft. Knox (June 1950)

Final Historical Report Covering Period D-Day to VE Day, Armored Fighting Vehicles and Weapons Section, HQ ETO US Army (1945)

History of the Armored Force, Command, and Center, Historical Section, Army Ground Forces (Study No. 27)

Organization, Equipment and Tactical Employment of Separate Tank Battalions, General Board, US Forces, European Theater (Study No. 50)

Organization, Equipment and Tactical Employment of Tank Destroyer Units, General Board, US Forces, European Theater (Study No. 60)

Tank Destroyer History, Historical Section, Army Ground Forces (Study No. 29)

Tank Gunnery, General Board, US Forces, European Theater (Study No. 53)

The Armored Group, General Board, US Forces, European Theater (Study No. 51)

The Separate Tank Battalion in Support of Infantry in River Crossing Operations in the ETO, Armored School, Ft. Knox (May 1950)

Published works

Bailey, Charles, *Faint Praise: American Tanks and Tank Destroyers during World War II* (Archon Books, 1983)

Blanchard, W. J., *Our Liberators: The Combat History of the 746th Tank Battalion during WWII* (Fenestra Books, 2003)

Elson, Aaron, *Tanks for the Memories: An Oral History of the 712th Tank Battalion from WWII* (Chi Chi Press, 1992).

Evans, Thomas, *Reluctant Valor: The 704th Tank Destroyer Battalion* (St. Vincent College, 1995)

Folkestad, William, *The View from the Turret: The 743rd Tank Battalion during World War II* (White Mane, 1996)

Gabel, Christopher, *Seek, Strike, and Destroy: US Army Tank Destroyer Doctrine in World War II* (US Army CGSC, 1985)

Gill, Lonnie, *Code Name: Harpoon, The Combat History of the 704th Tank Destroyer Battalion* (Baron Publishing, 1982)

Gill, Lonnie, *Tank Destroyer Forces—WWII* (Turner, 1992)

Heintzleman, Al, *The 741st Tank Battalion, D-Day to VE Day* (self-published, 1982)

Jensen, Marvin, *Strike Swiftly: The 70th Tank Battalion from North Africa to Normandy to Germany* (Presidio, 1997)

Rubel, George, *Daredevil Tankers: The Story of the 740th Tank Battalion* (self-published, 1945)

Wilson, Joe, Jr., *The 761st Black Panther Tank Battalion in World War II* (McFarland, 1999)

Yeide, Harry, *Steel Victory: The Heroic Story of America's Independent Tank Battalions at War in Europe* (Random House, 2003)

Index